Canadian Gardening's
NATURAL GARDENS

By LIZ PRIMEAU *and* THE EDITORS *of* CANADIAN GARDENING MAGAZINE
Consultants TREVOR *and* BRENDA COLE, FRANK KERSHAW

A FENN PUBLISHING COMPANY / MADISON PRESS BOOK

CANADIAN GARDENING'S
NATURAL GARDENS

ISBN 1-55168-288-5

A FENN PUBLISHING COMPANY/
MADISON PRESS BOOK

First Published in 2005

FENN PUBLISHING COMPANY LTD.
Bolton, Ontario, Canada

Distributed in Canada by

H. B. FENN AND COMPANY LTD.
Bolton, Ontario, Canada, L7E 1W2
www.hbfenn.com

Produced by

MADISON PRESS BOOKS
1000 Yonge Street, Suite 200
Toronto, Ontario, Canada
M4W 2K2

Printed in Singapore

Contents

Introduction

For some reason, the mere thought of creating a natural garden intimidates many gardeners. It's like composting — it sounds more complicated than it was ever meant to be. I must confess I felt that way until a few years ago, when it dawned on me that I was gardening naturally without realizing it. Most of my plants were native species like purple coneflower and black-eyed Susans, which I'd stuck to because they thrived in my garden without a lot of pampering — and for years, we'd been recycling kitchen and garden waste in the corner of the backyard.

I'm not a purist, though. Like many other natural gardeners, I also grow plants that aren't native to my Toronto-area garden, and its style is more organized than a natural landscape. There *are* purists in the natural gardening movement who prefer only gardens that copy nature's own style — like prairies or meadows. They also eschew "immigrant" plants that have become naturalized here, like Queen Anne's lace and oxeye daisies. And then there are those who believe that natural gardening means allowing nature to take over to see what you get. In my book, this is neglect.

If there's a debate, we sit squarely in the middle. To us, natural gardening is gardening with common sense: using plants that thrive in your soil and climate and avoiding harmful poisons that damage wildlife and beneficial insects. It also means designing a garden of your choice — whether it replicates nature or simply uses native plants and natural procedures in a more formal style. We hope that *Canadian Gardening's Natural Gardens* demystifies the subject for you and helps you plan a natural garden you'll enjoy.

Liz Primeau, Editor,
Canadian Gardening Magazine

CHAPTER ONE

Creating a
NATURAL
GARDEN

*A natural garden
mimics nature and offers us valuable lessons
about the mysterious and wondrous interactions
between all living things — right in our own
backyard. Unlike other gardens which we simply
stop to look at and admire, a natural garden invites
us to look into it and discover.*

What is a Natural Garden?

A natural garden is very closely tied to the existing terrain, climate and resilient native plant life of the garden site. The landscape is not shaped or altered artificially but simply enhanced to take advantage of the prevailing soil and climate conditions — a dry and sunny yard becomes a delightful meadow filled with sun-loving wildflowers, while a damp and shaded corner of the garden is transformed into a miniature woodland filled with airy ferns and dainty woodland flowers. Even traditional problem areas such as rock outcrops and steep slopes are turned into assets, woven effortlessly into the garden setting by a blanket of spreading ground covers.

Native plants, some introduced hardy perennials and ornamental grasses are the mainstay of a natural garden. As they grow and thrive, they crowd out undesirable weeds and require far less water and upkeep than traditional gardens and large expanses of lawn. But a natural garden is more than just a collection of native plants. It should be designed as an ecological community where plants attract other life forms such as birds, butterflies and frogs. A diversity of plants growing to different heights is ideal for accommodating the nesting, perching and hiding requirements of birds. A hollowed-out tree makes an excellent habitat for woodpeckers and flickers. And butterflies appreciate brightly colored meadow flowers such as blazing star, asters, goldenrod and butterfly weed.

At its best, a natural garden copies a scene from nature. A complete woodland garden, for example, includes a canopy of trees, a second layer of smaller trees and shrubs and a ground cover of wildflowers. Moss-covered logs, old stumps and a wood-chip trail reinforce the woodland image. A meadow garden, on the other hand, is an exposed landscape of sun-loving wildflowers and wild grasses tied together with simple mown paths. Plant form, texture, bark, fruits and seed heads all play an important role in adding to both the beauty and the utility of a natural garden. Just as in nature, the plants, insects and other wildlife that inhabit any natural garden are part of an ever-changing dynamic, as the hardiest plants establish themselves at the expense of others, and new species seed into an acceptable habitat.

A woodland garden filled with (from left) trilliums, yellow lady's slippers, dwarf columbine and white foamflowers.

But this joyful, natural chaos is not for everyone. To some people, a natural garden may appear untidy. It is a landscape where plants are left free and unchecked — to spill over edges and weave through each other as they realize their true growth potential — and where there is little evidence of the hard edges of paving, walls and structures. Nor is chemical control of insects or feeding of the soil necessary. Decomposing leaves add valuable, natural nutrients to the soil, while birds and beneficial insects such as spiders and ladybugs keep harmful pests at bay.

A natural garden offers us valuable lessons about the mysterious and wondrous interactions between all living things — right in our own backyard. Unlike other gardens which we simply stop to look at and admire, a natural garden invites us to look into it and discover....

Starting with Wildflowers

Blazing-star, wild columbine, wood poppy, butterfly weed — the names alone conjure up a fresh and unspoiled landscape that appeals to many of today's ecology-conscious gardeners. Whether you start with a small planting of trilliums under a single tree or dream of a large-scale meadow filled with hundreds of specimens, incorporating native plants, or wildflowers, in a garden setting is relatively easy to do. Providing you meet their soil and light requirements, they have an inbred tolerance of the local conditions and will thrive.

Wildflowers are also low-maintenance plants, which is especially appealing to gardeners with limited time. Planted in suitable habitats, wildflowers and some non-native perennials last for many years, for they are tenacious and have developed a resistance to disease, predators and climatic extremes. Instead of trying to change existing conditions, select plants that are suited to the climate, exposure, drainage and soil of your site. Since there are wildflowers suitable for all soils (sandy or clay, dry or boggy), choosing those plants that thrive in your soil type ensures a successful natural garden.

Jack-in-the-pulpit, blue phlox, wood poppies and ferns form the backbone of a woodland garden, while a meadow garden could be defined by wild lupines, bee balm and native lilies, and a wetland garden, by marsh marigolds, arrowhead and cardinal flower. Since plant distribution also reinforces mood, arrange plants as they

grow in the wild — in clumps and drifts, with the occasional single, accent plants — and limit the number of species. In fact, the best way to learn about wildflowers is to study them in their native habitats.

Once you decide on the wildflowers you would like to introduce to your garden, where do you obtain them? This is an ethical question that faces every natural gardener. While some native plants are protected by endangered species legislation, it is also illegal throughout Canada to take plants from parks, conservation areas and private property. Owners of cottages or country properties may transplant species within the confines of their land, and sometimes permission may be granted to move plants from private property where development is pending and the species may be destroyed. These rescue operations are often

advertised by botanical gardens, arboreta or local naturalist societies, and their staff or volunteers are on hand at the site to advise on what to collect, when to collect it and how to do it properly. Many native plants can only be moved successfully at a specific time of the year. Otherwise, leave wildflowers in their natural habitat for future generations to enjoy.

Collecting seed is less problematic, especially from full-sun species that set prolific seed. However, it is always best to obtain permission from the property owner before doing so. The preferred sources for wildflowers are nurseries that propagate their own plants (your local nursery association or botanical garden will be able to provide a list) or native plant societies, which hold plant sales and seed exchanges. Nursery-grown plants, propagated from collected seed, tend to have a denser, stronger root system, are more adaptable to cultivated soils and can be planted over a greater time frame than those dug up in the wild. They also provide the opportunity to experiment with native species not found naturally in your area.

When purchasing wildflowers from a nursery, purchase a substantial number of a few species and plant them in several potentially favorable areas — subtle variations in the microclimate in your garden can affect how well a species becomes established. In the right spot, the particular light, soil and moisture conditions might also enhance the growth of a plant and extend its bloom period.

For a list of Canadian native plant societies and other sources of information on wildflowers, see back of book.

CHAPTER TWO

WOODLAND GARDENS

*When we think of woodlands,
we imagine cool glades, delicate spring wildflowers, lush summer ferns
and the dappled play of sunlight and shadows. These are
restful places where texture, shape and pattern are as important
as the fleeting appearance of flowers.*

ature's woodlands are diverse and complex. They fuel our sense of adventure even as they satisfy our longing for calm. A woodland garden can evoke these feelings, too, whether it's a modest planting of wildflowers in a shady corner or a large, forested area at a rural retreat or cottage. Woodland gardens are also an excellent solution to the problem of encroaching shade in an established garden. Above all, they provide a wonderful opportunity for self-expression, and are a great way to get acquainted with nature.

The first step in making an effective woodland garden is to appreciate the spirit, look and mood of natural woodlands. Your own woodland should be a microcosm of nature, with its complexity developed on a smaller scale. It should also be a thoughtful exercise, involving the appreciation of nature, a basic understanding of woodland ecology and good horticultural practices. And while it may seem contradictory to "design" a natural garden, nature has discernible patterns that can be observed and copied.

Basic Structure

The first thing to observe about a natural woodland is its structure — it is formed in layers, with mounds of low wildflowers hugging the ground, mid-height shrubs rising gracefully above them and a canopy of both tall and smaller, understory trees providing shade and protection overhead. All play a role in nature, providing food and habitat for nesting birds and other wildlife, as well as leaves, evergreen needles and plant debris that break down when the season ends and enrich the soil.

A woodland also contains elements other than growing plants, such as logs, fallen branches and old stumps. Variations in texture, form and color also occur throughout the year, as they do in man-made gardens. The native maple trees are a good example. Stark and bare in winter, they take on a fresh green veil in spring, then change to the lush, deep-green foliage of summer and, finally, the brilliant leaves of autumn.

An old stump provides an ideal habitat for lush mayapple (Podophyllum peltatum).

Plants: The Building Blocks

It's important to remember that less is more in woodland gardens. Nature tends to use sheets of a small palette of plants rather than making a mini-botanical garden of many different species. Despite their delicate appearance, low to medium wildflowers with soft pastel colors and fine to medium textures are the backbone of the woodland garden. Plants like blue phlox (*Phlox divaricata*), foamflower (*Tiarella cordifolia*), dwarf bleeding hearts (*Dicentra eximia* and *D. formosa*), dwarf crested iris (*Iris cristata*) and wood ferns (*Dryopteris* spp.) create a woodland's image and mood.

▲ *Dwarf bleeding heart* (Dicentra eximia) *and yellow wood poppies* (Stylophorum diphyllum)

❧ Strategically massed, one species unites and tones down showier species and helps achieve a balance among plantings. A carpet of foamflowers, for example, knits together bolder and more vivid species such as Jack-in-the-pulpit (*Arisaema triphyllum*, sometimes labelled *A. atrorubens*) or wood poppies (*Stylophorum diphyllum*). The small size and dainty texture of low wildflowers encourage close viewing, which in turn enhances the intimate feeling of a woodland garden.

◀ *Foamflower*
(Tiarella cordifolia)

Baneberry ▶
(Astaea rubra)

◀ *White Trillium*
(Trillium grandiflorum)

Bunchberry ▶
(Cornus canadensis)

❧ As in nature, the change from one species to another in a woodland garden should be smooth and gradual. This is definitely not the place for rigid planting patterns — place plants so that one species gently flows into the next group along its edges.

❧ Combinations of wildflowers should mimic how they are distributed in nature — for example, hepatica usually appears in clumps, trilliums grow in sheets, baneberry and columbine are scattered throughout other plants. These patterns are the result of how plants propagate: seed-setters like columbine and baneberry sprout from seed carried and dropped by birds; the creeping roots of Canada mayflower (*Maianthemum canadense*) and barren strawberry (*Waldsteinia fragarioides*) form large, spreading colonies. Before you design your woodland garden, visit a nearby woods or conservation area and photograph

plants in their natural setting, and throughout the seasons, for later reference.

❧ You'll also want to include signature plants in your garden — species synonymous with woodlands in your part of the country, such as the white trillium (*Trillium grandiflorum*) in Ontario or the Pacific dogwood (*Cornus nuttallii*) in British Columbia. Each of these is its province's floral emblem, and their presence in your garden reinforces its regional identity.

❧ Other plants provide accents that evoke suspense, surprise and mystery. These include the late-blooming witch hazel (*Hamamelis virginiana*), appearing widely across the country, and the unusual green-dragon (*Arisaema dracontium*), a southern Ontario species named for its 8-inch (20 cm) spadix that looks like a dragon's tongue. Use accent plants sparingly or they'll lose their effect.

▲ *Mayapple* (Podophyllum peltatum)

▲ *Rose Twisted Stalk* (Streptopus roseus)　　　　　*Trout Lilies* (Erythronium *spp.*) ▼

❧ The many forms and textures among native Canadian wildflowers offer endless opportunities for plant combinations. The bold texture of bloodroot (*Sanguinaria canadensis*) or mayapple (*Podophyllum peltatum*) complements the dainty foliage of dwarf bleeding heart or the delicate maidenhair fern (*Adiantum pedatum*). The textural differences of plants affect the way we perceive the garden — fine textures recede from the viewer, while coarse textures come forward. A small woodland garden benefits from the use of more finely textured plants, which make it appear larger.

❧ Of course, plants indigenous to the area are preferred in woodland gardens, but because these plants aren't always available, using them exclusively may not be practical. In addition, the majority of our native woodland wildflowers are spring blooming, before the tree canopy leafs out and reduces the light intensity. To add interest later in the year, interplant non-natives such as hosta, astilbe, bergenia and foxglove with woodland wildflowers to fill the gaps left by spring bloomers such as trout lilies and Virginia bluebells. Ferns also help fill in the gaps. And don't overlook cultivated spring bulbs such as dainty checkered lilies (*Fritillaria meleagris*), muscari and snowdrops. In combination with wildflowers, they enhance the beauty of any woodland garden in spring (see p. 30).

HOSTAS MAKE *a* LUSH ADDITION
to any WOODLAND GARDEN

Although hostas aren't plants indigenous to Canada's woodlands, they are one of the most versatile of foliage plants — and that makes them especially popular for woodland or shade gardens.
❦ Their dramatic, tropical foliage is a great foil for shade-loving species, such as ferns and astilbes, and the varied leaf textures, which range from smooth to wavy and crinkly, add an interesting dimension to the garden. In the fall, the leaves on some cultivars turn a beautiful golden yellow and last until hard frost.
❦ Although there are about 40 species — *H. fortunei* and *H. ventricosa* are the more common ones — hostas cross-pollinate readily, producing many cultivars, and most nurseries and garden centers offer a wide selection. Some of the more striking cultivars, with equally catchy names that hint at foliage color or size, are 'Golden Sunburst', 'August Moon' and 'Blue Boy'.
❦ While hostas are grown mainly for their foliage, they also have attractive lily-like flowers that come in many sizes and shades of white, lavender, lilac and violet. These dancing bells light up the garden through summer and fall. Some are fragrant, especially *H. plantaginea* and its cultivars. Others, like 'Royal Standard', make excellent cut flowers.

shade-tolerant plants. Grow them with an intermediate-size shield fern (*Dryopteris* spp.) and *Astilbe* X *arendsii* 'Fanal', with its bright red flowers floating like torches above the muted green leaves of hostas.
❦ Numerous native wildflowers mix well with hostas — mayapple, wild ginger (*Asarum canadense*) and blue phlox are good candidates. If you want both color and foliage, combine sweet woodruff (*Galium odoratum*), a dainty white-flowering non-native ground cover, with green hostas.
❦ Avoid using variegated hostas in a woodland setting — they look unnatural.

CARE AND FEEDING

❦ Hostas are generally considered low-maintenance plants, provided they are grown in a loose, humus-fortified soil that retains moisture. Slightly acidic (pH 6.0 to 6.5) soils are to their liking. No fertilizing is necessary, provided new compost is added yearly.
❦ Although they are not invasive, hostas benefit from division when old clumps get too large. Divide in early spring or early fall.
❦ The color of the hosta foliage dictates the amount of shade it requires. Yellow leaves will take light, dappled shade, with some sun; green leaves do best in medium shade; while blue and blue-grey leaves need deep shade.
❦ Like other low-growing, shade-loving plants, hostas attract slugs and snails. To keep these in check, plant hostas in sharp, gritty soil or circle the plants with broken eggshells.

IN THE LANDSCAPE

❦ Bold, round hostas contrast well with the more upright, delicate foliage of ferns, astilbes and other

Woodland Ecology

A successful backyard woodland garden requires more than the right design and plants. You also need a basic understanding of woodland ecology.

SOIL

❧ The right soil is critical. Woodland plants favor friable, textured soils with good moisture retention that also allow sufficient air and moisture exchange. Soils should also be rich in nutrients and micro-organisms. Humus, the spongy-textured material comprising the organic matter that decays on the forest floor, contributes these qualities. The woodland gardener will have to add copious quantities of decayed leaves or compost, or leave the garden's leaf-fall to decay over time. Don't allow a dense layer to mat, however — it may smother spring-blooming wildflowers. Run your lawn mower over the leaves first to help break them up and speed decomposition.

❧ Most woodland plants favor a mildly acidic soil with a pH of 6.4 to 6.8, but there are regional and local exceptions. Plants on the west and east coasts, where conifers dominate, prefer more strongly acidic conditions with a pH as low as 5.5, whereas plants of the Great Lakes deciduous forest regions prefer soil only mildly acidic. While soil pH is important, texture is equally important. If you're not sure what kind of soil you have, have it tested.

❧ Soil containing a high percentage of clay holds excessive moisture and tends to become compacted; it is subject to frost heaving and stays cold late into the spring. This is not a desirable soil for woodland plants, unless you are able to amend it with ample quantities of peat moss and leaf mold.

❧ The preferred soil mix depends on where you live. In the Great Lakes region, you'll need two parts topsoil, one part leaf mold and one part coarse sand. A soil for the coniferous forest areas of the west coast and Atlantic Canada should be about 60 percent peat moss and 25 percent pine-needle compost, with the remainder coarse sand. If you are creating a woodland garden from scratch, it's critical that the top 6 inches (15 cm) be made up of the prepared mix, as this is the root zone of most woodland wildflowers.

LEAF MULCHES

❧ To maintain the right soil mix, apply 1-1/2 inches (4 cm) of leaf mulch in the early spring or late fall. Mulch buildup should not be a problem since wildflower roots grow into it and mulch gradually decomposes. Synthetic fertilizers aren't necessary, since a mulch provides enough nutrients; it also combats weeds and minimizes the need for supplemental watering, except during drought. And it retards soil erosion and provides the cool root runs favored by most woodland wildflowers.

SHADE

❧ Shade is another necessity, although it varies with the time of year, type of overhead trees, cloud cover and orientation of the property. Most wildflowers and shrubs do best in filtered or dappled shade, as opposed to the deep, continuous shade of pines and spruce. Low-branching trees may require some limbing-up and pruning to achieve filtered light and to improve air circulation.

Yellow Lady's Slipper (Cypripedium calceolus)

Pests *and* Problems

Once established, woodland gardens are generally considered low-maintenance. They are not, however, *no*-maintenance gardens.

❧ Fortunately, many woodland plants, such as ferns, have natural toxins that render them immune to most diseases and pests, but not to hot, dry weather. Some botanical gardens and arboreta irrigate their woodland gardens; all home gardeners need is a soaker hose for deep watering, particularly if there is competition from shallow-rooted maple and beech trees.

❧ Squirrels and rabbits can be a nuisance. Squirrels have been known to watch gardeners transplant dormant trilliums and trout lilies in the fall, then dig up the plants as soon as the gardener has gone indoors. Chicken wire or netting placed over the planted area should solve the problem. Discourage rabbits with wire tree guards, or spray rabbit repellent on the tree trunks. Scare away raccoons, which favor ponds, with a low-voltage electrical cable, available at water-garden supply stores.

❧ The damp conditions of a woodland garden also encourage slugs. Pick them off by hand or control with slug bait.

❧ Vigilant weed control is necessary in new woodland gardens until they become established, and invasive species such as Canada anemone (*Anemone canadensis*), garlic mustard (*Alliaria officinalis*) and black swallowwort (*Cynanchum nigrum*) can be troublesome. Mulch helps retard their invasion, but you may have to pull unwanted plants.

ADDING *to the* NATURAL LOOK

Man-made elements such as wood-chip or pine-needle paths, a split-log bench, natural-looking ponds with small streams or rocky waterfalls, and informal birdbaths are valuable additions to the backyard woodland garden — but they must never dominate the scene. They should be constructed of natural materials and be truly functional. In other words, pathways should lead somewhere, or provide access to plantings. Small, shallow preformed pools are acceptable if they are sunk in the ground, with soil, grass or bog plants hiding their edges. Ponds attract birds and frogs and reinforce the cool, serene image of the woodland garden. A brook or waterfall that is heard but not seen from all parts of the garden adds an air of mystery.

◄ Blue Phlox   *Virginia Bluebells ▲*

Woodland
Flowers

❧ WHITE TRILLIUM (*Trillium grandiflorum*) — 12- to 18-inch (30 to 45 cm) spring bloomer with spectacular, polar-white flowers. Ontario's floral emblem.

❧ WOOD POPPY (*Stylophorum diphyllum*) — 12- to 24-inch (30 to 60 cm) plant with butter-yellow flowers that bloom repeatedly.

❧ VIRGINIA BLUEBELLS (*Mertensia virginica*) — 12- to 24-inch (30 to 60 cm) spring bloomer with soft blue, bell-like flowers. Disappears after blooming, so consider planting with a companion such as ferns.

❧ BLUE PHLOX (*Phlox divaricata*) — 12- to 18-inch (30 to 45 cm) woodland plant with abundant violet-blue flowers and a creeping habit. Good for massing with other wildflowers.

❧ FOAMFLOWER (*Tiarella cordifolia*) — 6 to 8 inches (15 to 20 cm) tall, an excellent ground cover with frothy white flowers and maple leaf-shape foliage.

❧ FALSE SOLOMON'S SEAL (*Smilacina racemosa*) — a familiar sight in woodlands right across Canada, this 40-inch (1 m) arching plant has white flower plumes which resemble astilbe. Use as an accent plant on a sloping site where its form can be appreciated.

✿ NODDING TRILLIUM (*Trillium cernuum*) — 10- to 18-inch (25 to 45 cm) east-coast native with white to pinkish flowers hanging down below the leaves. Use as an accent or in clumps. Needs acid soil.

✿ TWINFLOWER (*Linnaea borealis*) — 4-inch (10 cm) ground cover with pink bell-shape flowers that grow in pairs. Looks especially good when planted in a mass.

✿ BLUE-BEAD LILY (*Clintonia borealis*) — 6- to 15-inch (15 to 40 cm) plant, with two or three shiny leaves at the base, yellow-green, bell-shape nodding flowers and dark purple berries.

✿ WINTERGREEN (*Gaultheria procumbens*) — 4-inch (10 cm) plant that spreads by creeping surface roots. Dark green, shiny oval leaves are aromatic. Small, white dangling flowers are followed by red berries.

✿ STARFLOWER (*Trientalis borealis*) — 4-inch (10 cm) ground cover with star-shape foliage and white flower petals. A striking and valuable addition to cool, damp woodlands.

▼ *Bleeding Heart*   *Twinflower* ▲

WESTERN CANADA

✿ WESTERN TRILLIUM (*Trillium ovatum*) — 12 to 18 inches (30 to 45 cm) tall with showy, large white flowers. An asset in any garden.

✿ DWARF BLEEDING HEART (*Dicentra formosa*) — 12 to 15 inches (30 to 40 cm) tall with dainty fern-like foliage and pink

or white pendant heart-shape flowers. Use as a ground cover.

✿ VANILLA LEAF (*Achlys triphylla*) — 12 to 24 inches (30 to 60 cm) tall, with distinct clover-shape foliage and a striking, white flower spike. A valuable accent plant or ground cover.

✿ REDWOOD SORREL (*Oxalis oregana*) — 4-inch (12 cm) high ground cover with clover-shape leaves and dainty pink flowers. Invasive — contain with a retainer strip.

LILY-OF-THE-VALLEY — HARBINGER *of* SPRING

The heady, sweet scent of lily-of-the-valley (*Convallaria majalis*) is a familiar one around the world each spring. Except for desert and polar areas, it thrives almost everywhere (to Zone 3 in Canada), survives under adverse conditions and is extremely easy to grow.

❧ Lily-of-the-valley reaches about 8 inches (20 cm) and grows from horizontal rhizomes that have upright buds called pips. It is ideal in moist, semi-shaded areas or under trees as a ground cover. A vigorous and invasive grower, it also looks good naturalized in large gardens or wooded areas with wildflowers, ferns and hostas.

❧ Bare-root pips should be planted in the fall (spring planting produces weaker first-year growth), but nursery plants can be set out anytime. Pips should be spaced 6 to 12 inches (15 to 30 cm) apart, depending on how long they are to be left before dividing, and planted 2 inches (5 cm) deep.

❧ If clumps are left undivided, lilies-of-the-valley will soon become dense and stop flowering. Dividing is best done in the fall; surplus pips can be potted and chilled for indoor forcing.

PRAIRIES

While woodland gardening is associated with the deciduous forests of the east and west coasts, the Prairies exhibit a rich diversity of habitats for native plants — from alpine meadows to aspen parkland, prairies and deciduous and boreal forests. As long as they have shade, Prairie gardeners have many opportunities to grow the woodland wildflowers below (which also thrive in Eastern Canada).

❧ JACK-IN-THE-PULPIT (*Arisaema triphyllum*, also labelled *A. atrorubens*) — 12- to 24-inch (30 to 60 cm) plant with a green or purplish-green hood projecting over a club-like spadix (the Jack, or preacher, in the pulpit). Foliage is large, with a tropical appearance. Red berries in fall.

❧ WILD COLUMBINE (*Aquilegia canadensis*) — grows 12 to 24 inches (30 to 60 cm) tall, with delicate, dissected foliage and drooping red, bell-shape spurred flowers in spring that attract hummingbirds.

❧ WILD GERANIUM (*Geranium maculatum*) — showy and robust 12- to 27-inch (30 to 70 cm) plant with attractive, 5-petalled, pinkish-blue to rose-purple flowers in late spring. Five-lobed foliage turns reddish-purple in the fall.

❧ BLOODROOT (*Sanguinaria canadensis*) — 8 to 12 inches (20 to 30 cm) tall, with delicate 8- to 10-petalled white flowers that open in the sun and close at night, generally in early spring.

❧ WOODLAND SUNFLOWER (*Helianthus divaricatus*) — 30 to 45 inches (80 to 120 cm) tall, with striking yellow daisy-like summer flowers. Seeds are a source of food for birds.

❧ WHITE WOODLAND MILKWEED (*Ascelepias exaltata*) — 35- to 60-inch (90 to 150 cm) plant with drooping clusters of white flowers tinged with lavender or green. Flowers in late July.

Jack-in-the-pulpit

▲ *Wild Geranium*

Bloodroot (left) with dainty Sweet Woodruff (Galium odoratum) ▼

Indispensable Ferns

Elegant ferns, with their luxurious dissected foliage, impart an air of lightness and grace to a woodland garden. Their varying shades of green also soothe the eye and enhance the mood of peace and tranquility.

❧ The cool, moist climate of many parts of Canada is ideal for growing both native and non-native ferns. In Ontario alone, there are 68 native species — with 55 in British Columbia, and more than 100 in the rest of the country.

❧ In the wild, ferns are found in forests, dry exposed pastures and logged-over areas, along the edges of streams and ponds, and tucked in the crevices of rocks. Transplanted to a garden setting, they thrive where conditions are similar to their native habitat, such as the cool shade of a grove of trees, or along the north side of a wall or the edge of a pond.

❧ Plant ferns at a distance that is approximately equal to their eventual height. This not only gives them room to grow but also promotes good air circulation.

FERNS IN COMBINATION

With their dark green foliage, ferns contrast beautifully with the flowers, fruit and leaves of other plants.

❧ For light shade, try ostrich ferns (*Matteuccia struthiopteris*) with orange daylilies (*Hemerocallis* spp.), pink *Malva alcea fastigiata* or woodland sunflowers (*Helianthus divaricatus*).

❧ A mass planting of bulblet or marsh ferns (*Thelypteris palustris*) with forget-me-nots (*Myosotis scorpioides*) and yellow cowslip primula (*Primula veris*) makes a dramatic statement in a damp corner of the garden.

❧ Ferns are also delightful with many wildflowers such as trilliums, Virginia bluebells (*Mertensia virginica*), wild columbine (*Aquilegia canadensis*) and foamflower (*Tiarella cordifolia*).

❧ Combining ferns with bold foliage plants such as hostas, Jack-in-the-pulpit (*Arisaema triphyllum*), lady's mantle (*Alchemilla mollis*) and bergenias underscores the fine texture of the ferns. For a more subtle effect, pair ferns with plants that also have delicate, fern-like foliage, such as bleeding heart (*Dicentra formosa* or *D. eximea*), astilbe, Jacob's ladder (*Polemonium caeruleum*), meadow rue (*Thalictrum* spp.) and goatsbeard (*Aruncus* spp.).

DESIGNING WITH FERNS

Ferns are excellent ground covers, filling the gap left by wildflowers and spring bulbs that disappear shortly after blooming. They shade out weeds, keep the soil cool and carry the lushness of spring to the summer

garden. The varied size, form, color and texture of ferns also makes them a versatile design element in the garden.

🌿 The impressive size of even a few ferns adds presence to a small garden.

🌿 Crown or clump-forming species — such as ostrich (*Matteuccia struthiopteris*), Goldie's (*Dryopteris goldiana*) and western sword (*Polystichum munitum*) — and interrupted ferns (*Osmunda claytoniana*), with their upright form and size, make ideal accents on their own or in combination with other plants.

🌿 Lacy maidenhair ferns (*Adiantum pedatum*) and the crested, tassled forms of lady ferns (*Athyrium* spp.) add a delicate texture to the garden.

🌿 Japanese painted fern (*Athyrium nipponicum* 'Pictum'), with its silvery fronds and red stems, provides a dramatic note in a planting of colorful wildflowers.

🌿 The unusual fertile fronds of the cinnamon (*Osmunda cinnamomea*) and sensitive (*Onoclea sensibilis*) ferns stand out in a garden like bold exclamation marks. As with any garden accent, these plants make the biggest impact if they are used sparingly and given enough room to look their best.

🌿 Ferns also make excellent edging plants along paths and beside streams. Choose hardy, medium-size plants such as Christmas (*Polystichum acrostichoides*), shield (*Dryopteris* spp.), deer (*Blechnum spicant*) and Braun's holly (*Polystichum braunii*) ferns.

Tall ostrich, interrupted or royal ferns, grouped with equally tall flowering plants, create the striking illusion that the ferns are in bloom. For maximum impact, design the planting so that there are companion flowers for each season: consider fingerleaf rodgersia (*Rodgersia aesculifolia*) with its white, astilbe-like flowers in early summer; rusty foxglove (*Digitalis ferruginea*) and the aptly named white goatsbeard (*Aruncus* spp.) for summer interest; the lovely Japanese yellow bellflower (*Kirengeshoma palmata*) in late summer; and black cohosh (*Cimicifuga racemosa*) with its spires of white flowers in the fall.

CARE AND FEEDING

Despite their delicate appearance, ferns are hardy and reliable, provided they are properly planted in appropriate habitats. Woodland ferns thrive in modest shade and in moist, slightly acidic, humus-rich soils.

Since ferns are heavy feeders, start with an organic-rich soil composed of almost equal parts leaf mold, topsoil and well-rotted manure to a depth of at least 10 inches (25 cm).

The application of a shredded bark or leaf mulch in early spring or fall helps conserve moisture, protects against frost heaving and contributes nutrients to the soil.

Ferns that thrive in acidic soils benefit from a mulch of oak leaves or pine needles. For lime-loving ferns — such as Christmas, maidenhair and polypody — add a yearly light dusting of bonemeal to the soil.

Many ferns require division every three to five years depending on the species. Creeping ferns, which spread by root runners, send up new offspring which compete with parent plants for nutrients and water. Divide these with a sharp spade in early spring, just as the fiddleheads show, and plant at the same height. Water well for the first few weeks.

Since ferns contain natural toxins in their tissues, insects and disease are seldom a problem.

FERNS *for the* GARDEN

GREAT LAKES REGION

CHRISTMAS FERN (*Polystichum acrostichoides*) — grows up to 24 inches (60 cm) tall, with lustrous, dark green arching fronds. This native prefers rich, limy soil and woodland conditions, and does best in shade or semi-shade. Provides year-round appeal and mixes well with many wildflowers.

BULBLET FERN (*Cystopteris bulbifera*) — a graceful fern, 10 to 24 inches (25 to 60 cm) tall, with a tufted form and narrow leaves. Prefers a drier, lime-rich soil and semi-shade in rockeries and around waterfalls and streams. Reproduction is by small bulblets, produced on the lower side of the fronds, that drop to the ground and grow into new ferns.

ROYAL FERN (*Osmunda regalis*) — a tall, upright native with regal bearing and unique locust-like leaflets. It reaches a height of 48 inches (120 cm) and requires wet, acidic soil and full or partial sun. Useful around ponds, lakes and stream edges.

JAPANESE PAINTED FERN (*Athyrium nipponicum* 'Pictum') — a 12- to 24-inch (30 to 60 cm) non-native with delicate arching fronds and a unique purple-grey color. It thrives in slightly acidic, humus-rich soil and prefers full or partial shade. Use as an accent, edging plant or in combination with bulbs or other shade plants.

OSTRICH FERN (*Matteuccia struthiopteris*) — this is one of the better-known native ferns. It grows up to 60 inches (150 cm) tall and has arching, shuttlecock-shape, dark green tapered fronds. Requires rich, slightly acid, dampish soil and is commonly used as a tall ground cover in semi-shade.

❧ MAIDENHAIR FERN (*Adiantum pedatum*) — one of the most beautiful textured ferns, it grows 12 to 24 inches (30 to 60 cm) tall, with fan-shaped fronds borne on ebony stalks. Does best in moist, lime-rich soil. Use as an accent.

(*Note: the ferns listed for the Prairies and East Coast also thrive in the Great Lakes Region.*)

WEST COAST

❧ AUTUMN OR JAPANESE RED SHIELD FERN (*Dryopteris erythrosora*) — a compact mound shape, 12 to 24 inches (30 to 60 cm) tall, with copper-pink fronds that mature into rich green leaflets overlaid with hues of red and copper. This non-native prefers moist, humus-rich soil and partial shade.

❧ WESTERN SWORD FERN (*Polystichum munitum*) — a 36- to 60-inch (90 to 150 cm) common west-coast native that looks like an overgrown Christmas fern with leathery, dark green fronds. Thrives in semi-shade and coniferous woods, and is easy to grow.

❧ OAK FERN (*Gymnocarpium dryopteris*) — 6 to 12 inches (15 to 30 cm) tall, a delicate triangular-shape fern with fast-spreading underground roots that produce large colonies in acid, rocky soil. Frequently used as a ground cover or edging plant in west coast gardens.

❧ LADY FERN (*Athyrium filix-femina*) — a 36- to 48-inch (90 to 120 cm) native that thrives in moist woods around lakes and along streams. Light green foliage matures into many small, darker green leaflets that give it a delicate air. Its dense mound shape makes it perfect for massing with wildflowers or as a backdrop planting. Can also be found throughout the Great Lakes Region.

❧ JAPANESE HOLLY FERN (*Cyrtomium falcatum*) — 12 to 24 inches (30 to 60 cm) tall, with leathery, dark green foliage that resembles Oregon grape (*Mahonia aquifolium*). Does well in a range of soils, and sun or shade conditions.

❧ PARSLEY FERN (*Cryptogramma crispa*) — this small, 6- to 12-inch (15 to 30 cm) rock-loving native has parsley-like fronds and a lovely tussock shape. It prefers semi-shade and slightly moist, acidic soils. Plant in the cracks and crevices of shaded rockeries.

❧ ALASKAN FERN (*Polystichum angulare*) — narrow fronds up to 24 inches (60 cm) tall, with feathery, dark green leaflets. Prefers the moist, acid soil found under conifers.

❧ DEER FERN (*Blechnum spicant*) — 12 to 36 inches (30 to 90 cm) tall, this tussock-shape beauty has upright fertile fronds with a distinctive air. Prefers moist, acid, coniferous-forest soil and full or partial shade. Striking as a ground cover under rhododendrons.

PRAIRIES

❧ BRACKEN (*Pteridium aquilinum*) — a somewhat coarse, dark green, three-parted fern that grows to 36 inches (90 cm) and tolerates full sun and gritty, acidic soil. Useful as a hardy ground cover and for stabilizing soil on rural and cottage properties. Can be invasive.

❧ SENSITIVE FERN (*Onoclea sensibilis*) — has leathery, light green, triangular fronds, grows 24 to 36 inches (60 to 90 cm) tall and does well in full sun or light shade, provided it has ample moisture and humus-rich, alkaline soil. Dies back with the first frost. Its coarse-toothed leaflets contrast well with the round leaves of hostas.

❧ INTERRUPTED FERN (*Osmunda claytoniana*) — a somewhat coarse, robust fern with fertile spores midway up the stalk of the fronds. Does well in full or partial shade and drier, alkaline soil. At 24 to 48 inches (60 to 120 cm) tall, it makes a striking foundation planting.

EAST COAST

❧ CINNAMON FERN (*Osmunda cinnamomea*) — this strong, upright fern reaches a height of 72 inches (180 cm) and has distinct club-like, cinnamon-colored fertile fronds in the spring. It thrives in partial shade and rich, damp soil and makes a striking accent around streams or pools.

❧ MARGINAL SHIELD FERN (*Dryopteris marginalis*) — a native evergreen fern that grows to 24 inches (60 cm) and prefers semi-shade and dry to moderately moist, alkaline soil. With leathery, dark green fronds that form graceful clumps, it offers winter interest and is particularly effective for massing with wildflowers and other shade plants.

BULBS *in a* NATURAL SETTING

*T*here is nothing like
a sea of sunny yellow daffodils, crocuses
and grape hyacinths to set our winter-weary
spirits soaring. We delight in how freely they
grow, planted as if by the hand of nature to
bloom and spread at will.

Many bulbs can be naturalized in meadows, woodlands and grass, under trees or spilling through flowerbeds.

Naturalizing bulbs — establishing a self-sustaining colony of plants that grow and multiply as they would in nature — is one of the prettiest and most effortless ways to enjoy them in a natural garden. Many of the bulbs used formally in our gardens, such as tulips and daffodils, are bred from species native to woodlands, meadows and grasslands around the Mediterranean, from Portugal and Spain through to Asia Minor. English gardeners, recognizing these origins, have long used bulbs in natural settings on country estates and in botanical gardens. In most of Canada, the warm, moist springs and hot, dry summers duplicate the natural climate of many bulbs, making much of the country ideal for planting and enjoying bulbs in a natural setting. Although most bloom in the spring, there are some summer- and fall-flowering bulbs that also naturalize well, such as species lilies and autumn crocus (*Colchicum autumnale*).

To naturalize bulbs, select those that multiply and spread rapidly by seed; some hybrids aren't good candidates because they bloom for only a few years and gradually decline. Others with large blooms in vivid colors are unsuitable in a natural setting. Although naturalized plants require little care once they are established, you need to give some thought to where and how to plant them before you start. Bulbs should be planted in areas large enough to let them multiply and, if planted in a lawn, where grass can be left uncut until their foliage ripens after blooming.

Getting Started

❧ Choose a site with fertile, well-drained soil. Since your goal is to make the area look as if the bulbs grow there by happy chance, you can either scatter large stones and let them randomly mark the spots where bulbs will be planted (this works best for small plantings, in small areas) or you can simply dig the holes at random. Dig to the correct depth for each bulb, mix bonemeal into the bottom of each hole and position the bulb. Cover the bulbs with soil and tamp in place. Water the area and mulch, if necessary.

❧ Plant in quantity. It may take several years to achieve the impact of a sea of daffodils or a river of grape hyacinths, so start with a dozen of each type and let them spread. Try to add to the area each year.

❧ Remove spent flowers but leave foliage intact. Bulbs rely on their leaves to gather the nourishment needed to create next year's blooms. Some bulbs die down quickly but it may take six to eight weeks for the leaves of others to ripen or yellow. Only then should they be removed or mown. If leaves are removed sooner, the bulbs may not flower the following year, or may die altogether.

Bulbs *in a* Woodland Garden

Woodland bulbs prefer neutral soil, good drainage and light shade. They're at their best bordering a path or spreading under trees that come into leaf after the bulbs bloom.

✿ Many woodland bulbs, such as snowdrops (*Galanthus* spp.) and blue squill (*Scilla siberica*), bloom in early spring and warm the hearts of gardeners long before the ground thaws. They are particularly striking against the light bark of beech, serviceberry, white birch and magnolia trees.

✿ Bulbs that flower later in the spring, such as Spanish bluebells (*Hyacinthoides hispanica*), Greek windflower (*Anemone blanda*), snakeshead fritillary (*Fritillaria meleagris*) and trumpet daffodils, are effective naturalized under taller shrubs or

Snakeshead Fritillary (Fritillaria meleagris 'Aphrodite')

❧

mixed with perennials. Try Spanish bluebells under a copse of redbud (*Cercis canadensis*), or grape hyacinths (*Muscari* spp.) with white foamflower (*Tiarella cordifolia*) in large informal drifts.

❧ Bulbs naturalized beside ponds and streams soften their edges and add splashes of color.

❧ When selecting bulbs to naturalize in a woodland or shady area, choose strong, quality bulbs that will be able to withstand the competition from tree roots for nutrients and moisture.

❧ To mask the yellowing foliage of early-blooming bulbs, plant them close to tree trunks and add a screen of ferns, hostas or bulbs that bloom later in the season or in early summer, such as the beautiful turk's-cap lily (*Lilium martagon*) or summer snowflake (*Leucojum aestivum*).

❧ Protected areas that thaw early provide an ideal microclimate for extending the bloom period. Bulbs will often flower up to two weeks earlier than the same species planted in an exposed area. You can also extend the bloom time by planting later-flowering cultivars of the same species.

PLANTING WOODLAND BULBS

❧ Bulbs can either be planted randomly or in long drifts of 50 or more bulbs. Larger bulbs, such as hybrid daffodils and tulips, should be planted at least 8 inches (20 cm) deep and at least 6 to 8 inches (15 to 20 cm) apart; plant smaller bulbs, such as snowdrops and scilla, 4 inches (10 cm) deep and about 3 inches (8 cm) apart.

❧ Planting at the correct depth is particularly important. Bulbs planted too close to the surface are susceptible to frost heaving; those planted too deeply will be weakened as they struggle to break the surface.

❧ Plant spring-blooming bulbs in the early fall when the soil temperature is between 8 and 15°C (45 and 60°F), so there is sufficient time for root development before the ground freezes. This is especially true for narcissus, snakeshead fritillary and trout lilies (*Erythronium* spp.), which are slow to root.

❧ If you plant bulbs in well-drained, humus-rich soil and allow leaf decomposition to add nutrients to the soil, fertilizing is not necessary.

❧ Squirrels, chipmunks and mice unearth most bulbs, given the chance. Narcissi are usually left alone because they are planted too deep to reach. Other bulbs can be protected in baskets made of chicken wire that allow the leaf and flower bud through but discourage digging animals. Leaf mulch and other forest litter over the planted area help disguise and protect the site — although squirrels seem to smell bulbs underground!

Bulbs *in* Grassy Areas

Plantings in grass should be bold, sweeping compositions in the shape of long drifts or crescents, thickest at the start and thinning out at the end. Keep to the same species or cultivar in each drift and stress distinct, vivid colors.

❧ Since grass can't be mown until bulb foliage ripens — sometimes as long as six to eight weeks after bulbs bloom — choose a site on your property where long grass isn't a problem or plant early-flowering bulbs, such as species crocus or snowdrops.

❧ Roadside embankments are an ideal natural site for bulbs. A planting pattern that follows the contours of the land is most effective. Trumpet daffodils are among the most striking flowers in this setting; interplant them with daylilies (*Hemerocallis* spp.), which emerge from the ground just in time to hide the ripening leaves of the spent daffodils.

PLANTING BULBS IN GRASS

❧ The size of the area, coarseness of the grass and existing soil and drainage conditions all play a part in determining how bulbs should be planted in grass.

❧ In small areas with loose soil, simply remove a plug of turf and soil with a trowel or bulb planter, insert the bulb, firm the soil around it and replace the plug. The planting depth and the spacing between bulbs are the same as for woodland bulbs (see p. 35).

Planting a large area is labor-intensive. You'll need to remove large sections of sod (consider renting a sod cutter) and either plant bulbs with a bulb planter or remove the soil to the proper planting depth, set out the bulbs and replace the soil. Once the planting is complete, replace the sod and water thoroughly.

Use only strong, quality bulbs for a good show of blooms the following year. Once established, bulbs naturalized in grass require only modest fertilizer and water. Since bulbs planted in grass are competing for plant foods at a time when the grass is in active growth, apply a 5-10-10 soluble fertilizer as soon as flowering is finished to help the bulb form next year's flower. Avoid lawn fertilizers high in nitrogen (represented by the first number in the formula) until the bulb foliage has started to turn brown.

MAINTENANCE

Remove spent flowers on narcissus to produce stronger bulbs and to allow the foliage to ripen more quickly. Leave the flower stalks; they help to feed the bulb. Smaller bulbs, such as *Chionodoxa*, *Scilla* and *Eranthis* species, spread rapidly by seed and shouldn't be deadheaded. Division of bulbs is not necessary.

Larger bulbs, such as daffodils, benefit from bulb division every four or five years since crowding results in fewer, smaller blooms. Dig up the bulbs when the leaves start to turn brown, divide the crowded clumps into individual bulbs and replant immediately at the correct spacing.

Bulbs *for* Woodlands *and* Grass

❧ BLUE SQUILL (*Scilla siberica*) — a short, 4- to 5-inch (10 to 13 cm) plant with striking, Persian blue, bell-shape flowers and grassy foliage in early spring. Spreads quickly by seed and is delightful for naturalizing under trees, rockeries and banks, especially with glory of the snow and miniature narcissus. Hardy to Zone 3.

❧ SPANISH BLUEBELLS (*Scilla campanulata*) — a late-spring bloomer with numerous blue, pink or white bell-shape flowers on 16-inch (40 cm) stems. Favors light shade and moist, humus-rich soil. Dramatic when planted under redbuds, serviceberry, or pink and red rhododendrons. It makes a good edging plant along paths when interplanted with hostas and ferns or other plants that can take over when the bluebells have finished flowering. Increases rapidly by division or seed to form substantial colonies. Hardy to Zone 5.

❧ SNAKESHEAD FRITILLARY (*Fritillaria meleagris*) — a 12- to 14-inch (30 to 35 cm) plant with interesting purple to brown-checkered or white nodding, bell-shape flowers and slender, grassy foliage. Blooms mid- to late spring and favors moist meadows and woodlands. A native of England's wet meadows, it is readily available and easy to grow. Hardy to Zone 4.

❧ GRAPE HYACINTH (*Muscari* spp.) — noted for its profuse, fragrant blue flowers on 6- to 8-inch (15 to 20 cm) stems. Ideal for naturalizing in short grass, in woodlands, under shrubs and in rockeries. Particularly striking with white trillium and foamflower. Self-seeds quickly, and grows well in sun or light shade. Hardy to Zone 3.

❧ TROUT LILY (*Erythronium* spp.) — this lily has beautiful nodding, lemon-yellow flowers with slightly mottled leaves. Plants grow to 10 inches (25 cm) and require moist, humus-rich soil. Excellent for massing in large clumps with white trilliums and other wildflowers. Buy fresh bulbs and plant as soon as possible to prevent them from drying out. Sometimes difficult to obtain in large quantities. Hardy to Zone 5.

Blue Squill

❧ GREEK ANEMONE OR WINDFLOWER (*Anemone blanda*) — beautiful white, pink or blue daisy-like flowers with dissected, fern-like foliage. Blooms in mid- to late spring. These 4- to 6-inch (10 to 15 cm) plants spread quickly by seed and require fairly rich woodland soil. Often used as an underplanting below azaleas and rhododendrons as well as other spring-flowering trees and shrubs. Soak tubers the night before planting to ensure success. Hardy to Zone 5.

❧ SUMMER SNOWFLAKE (*Leucojum aestivum*) — a 16-inch (40 cm) tall plant that looks like a giant snowdrop with grassy foliage and fragrant, dainty, flared white flowers. Does best in full sun or part shade, in humus-rich, moisture-retentive soil. Often used along streams or under shrubs in a border. Hardy to Zone 5.

❧ AUTUMN CROCUS (*Colchicum autumnale*) — these 4- to 6-inch (10 to 15 cm) plants bloom in the fall in an array of colors from white to mauve and amethyst. Similar in appearance to spring-blooming crocuses but larger and much showier, they do well in woodland areas but the large leaves produced in spring make them difficult to grow in a lawn. Hardy to Zone 4.

❧ DAFFODILS AND NARCISSUS (*Narcisuss* hybrids) — available in a range of heights and flower shapes, narcissus are invaluable for naturalizing. The large forms, in shades of yellow, pink, white and cream, thrive in well-drained but moist soil and in sun to dappled shade. Smaller varieties can be planted in grass either alone or mixed with earlier flowering bulbs such as the blue squill. Hardy to Zone 4.

❧ CROCUS (*Crocus* spp.) — look best when planted in drifts of one color. Use the small-flower species (and their hybrids) in preference to the large-flowered Dutch crocus which flowers earlier and dies down faster. The crocus often called Golden Bunch (*C. ancyrensis*) is one of the first to flower and will spread slowly by seed if conditions suit it.

❧ SNOWDROPS (*Galanthus nivalis*) — often blooming before the snow has completely melted, snowdrops are the true harbinger of spring. The single, nodding flowers are carried on 4-inch (10 cm) wiry stems. They grow best in light shade but will also survive planted in a lawn. Hardy to Zone 5.

❧ GLORY OF THE SNOW (*Chionodoxa lucillae*) — early-blooming blue, star-like flowers with white centers are clustered on 4-inch (10 cm) stems. Grows well in lawns and seeds freely under trees and shrubs. Hardy to Zone 3.

❧ TULIPS (*Tulipa* spp.) — while the hybrid garden tulips are not well-suited to a woodland garden, a few of the small species will thrive when planted close to the edge where they get better light. *T. tarda*, an early-spring bloomer, has up to eight yellow flowers, edged in white, on each bulb and grows only 8 inches (20 cm) tall. It multiplies fast and will seed itself. The slower-growing *T. pulchella* is similar in size, with mauvish-pink flowers. The wood tulip, *T. sylvestris*, tolerates more shaded conditions, produces bright yellow flowers on 12-inch (30 cm) stems in late spring and self-seeds.

❧ WINTER ACONITE (*Eranthis hyemalis*) — will often bloom with the snowdrops, grows well in dappled shade and seeds itself freely. Bright yellow buttercup-like flowers sit on a ruff of lacy foliage. Buy this as soon as bulbs appear in garden stores and soak newly purchased bulbs (which look like little pieces of leather) overnight before planting. Hardy to Zone 4.

▲ *Greek Anemone or Windflower*   *Crocus* ▼

GARDENS
in the SUN

*B*lack-eyed Susans,
wild bergamot, butterfly weed, orange daylilies,
dotted blazing star.... The flowers of sun-drenched
summer meadows, prairies and country roadsides
are equally at home in your garden — provided
you give them lots of sunshine, and let nature be
the inspiration for your garden design.

MEADOW LANDSCAPES

*Just as woodlands evoke a mood of coolness and tranquility,
meadows warm us with memories of bright summer wildflowers
and soothing green grasses.*

Creating your own wildflower meadow requires planning and work — as well as familiarity with the conditions under which meadow plants thrive — but the finished landscape is more than worth the effort. If your property isn't large enough to support a true meadow, you can still incorporate the random beauty of a meadow planting in a smaller setting, such as a weekend property or a residential backyard, by interspersing islands of meadow flowers with areas of mown lawn or making them the centerpiece of a flowerbed in a sunny part of the garden. In fact, many of the perennials traditionally found in a garden — such as asters, black-eyed Susan, wild bergamot and purple coneflower — are native meadow plants.

Meadows can be wet or dry and can have almost any soil type as long as it is neither waterlogged nor too rich. The most important consideration is sunlight; to thrive, any meadow or meadow-style planting must have at least six hours of full sun per day, so choose an area with little or no tree cover nearby.

As well as an open field, ideal sites for a meadow garden include a dry sunny bank, a rocky or gravelly slope, a fence line along a country property, or the sunny corner of an urban backyard. A meadow's composition and growth depend on where it is, and on the prevailing conditions. Regional differences in soil, rainfall, drainage and climate dictate which plants will grow best in a given area.

A monarch butterfly perches motionless on a flat-topped cluster of stiff goldenrod.

Meadow Plants

Meadow plants fall into two categories — grasses and wildflowers. Unlike flowers in a woodland garden, which bloom mainly in the spring, meadow flowers are at their best in summer and fall. And, in contrast to the softer pastel shades of woodland plants, many of the species that thrive in the sun are bright red, orange and yellow. The numerous species of grasses and wildflowers offer endless color and texture combinations, and the high visibility and profusion of the bright flowers attracts many insects, including dozens of different butterflies.

Like native plants in other habitats, meadow plants only depend on rainfall and the nutrients available in the soil to meet their needs.

Before deciding on which plants to grow where, study various native species in their natural habitat to see how, and with what other plants, they grow. Some wildflowers, such as northern bedstraw (*Galium boreale*), grow in large sheets while others, such as black-eyed Susan (*Rudbeckia hirta*), thrive in clumps. There are also some plants, like the wood lily (*Lilium philadelphicum*), that grow as individual specimens and serve as accents, standing out in a sea of other flowers. Whatever the pattern of growth, the interrelationship between species is also important. A meadow is an interdependent community of plants and each wildflower relies on the others around it. Taller plants, for example, may be affected by the absence of lower associated species — including grasses, which provide support — by being blown down in a strong wind.

As nice as wildflowers are, they need the foil of grasses to set them off. The changing patterns of growth in grasses — from the first flush of soft green, through the flower stems swaying in the breeze, to the rich brown tones of fall — add interest to a meadow year-round. Some wildflowers, especially in the midwest, have a symbiotic relationship with grasses and cannot grow without them. Be sure that any seed mix you buy contains several species of native grass. Ornamental grasses, such as those used in more formal gardens, can be included in a bed of meadow wildflowers but should be used in moderation.

Planting *your own* Meadow

If you are planning to convert a residential front lawn or backyard into a full-blown meadow, be sure to let your neighbors know before you start. Not everyone is ready for the leap from manicured lawn to carefree wildflowers and grasses — and you may need to reassure the neighborhood that you're not about to create an eyesore, and will control what you plant. Some municipalities have bylaws on controlling native species they consider weeds. Before you start, you may need to talk to your elected representative and obtain a waiver.

Many wildflower and native grass seeds need a period of cold to germinate well, so the best time to sow a meadow or prairie garden is in the fall, after the majority of migrating birds have left, but before the soil freezes. You will lose a little seed to resident birds and mice but losses should be minimal. Fall sowing will give the best germination and, because of the moisture in the soil, the seedlings will grow faster and you will have to water less. Failing this, mix the seed with a little damp sand and keep it over winter in the refrigerator at a temperature below 41°F (5°C); sow as early as soil conditions allow in spring (see sowing instructions, next page).

Preparing *the* Site

Despite the promises made on some packets of wildflower seeds, there's more work to creating a meadow than simply scattering the seeds over the garden and letting nature take its course. Planting a meadow is almost like planting a lawn from scratch — and that means preparing the soil first, to ensure good drainage and aeration so that seeds will germinate and grow. If you are replacing a lawn with a meadow, you will need to remove the sod before preparing the ground.

❧ Dig the area over to a minimum of 6 inches (15 cm) deep, removing all large stones, debris and any large roots. Unless the soil is very poor, it is not necessary to

Wood Lily (Lilium philadelphicum)

add soil amendments; these only encourage excessive growth. If the soil was supporting lawn, it will grow meadow plants. Very poor, sandy soils can be improved by the addition of compost or peat moss, while heavy clay soils need sharp sand to improve their drainage, along with some organic matter to add texture.

❧ After digging, rake the soil more or less level. The area should then be watered to encourage the weed seeds near the surface to germinate. As soon as there is a good crop of weed seedlings showing, hoe the soil with a Dutch (scuffle) hoe to kill them. Hoeing will disturb the soil surface and bring more weed seeds up to germinate. Ideally, this cycle of germination and hoeing should be done for a full season — but at least do it several times before actually sowing your wildflower mix. After the final hoe, allow the weeds to die, then rake the surface until the soil is quite fine, trying not to bring fresh soil, and weed seeds, to the surface.

Planting *and* Maintenance

Sowing the seed for your meadow is the easy part. For best results, use a quality commercial mix suited to your site and hardy to your area.

❧ Mix seed in a bowl with fine, dry sand at a rate of five parts sand to one part seed (using sand ensures an even distribution of seed). Divide the mix of sand and seed into two equal portions. Broadcast one half by hand over the prepared area, then broadcast the other half at right angles. This ensures an even coverage. Very lightly rake the seed into the surface, using a fan-type lawn rake and, unless you have very heavy soil, lightly roll the area. A light mulch will keep the seeds from washing away.

❧ Water thoroughly with a fine spray and rope off the area to stop pets and people from walking over it. You will need to water every two or three days (depending on rainfall) until the plants are well established. Because you are sowing a mix of seeds, not everything will germinate at the same time — so don't be too eager to stop watering. There may be tiny seedlings of a showy plant just starting to grow. Meadows can also be started from nursery-grown material, planted randomly, but this is expensive — especially for large areas. Transplants are ideally suited to smaller areas or in flower beds where meadow wildflowers are used as an accent planting.

A meadow grown from seed evolves slowly. The first summer, there will be mainly annual species in bloom, but these will gradually die out over the first few years as the perennials take over and crowd them out. It will be two to three years before your meadow matches the photo on the seed packet but, once it comes into its own, you'll have a carefree, natural garden that celebrates the sun.

Meadow Flowers *for your* Garden

Many sun-loving native plants, such as black-eyed Susans and purple coneflower, grow throughout Canada and make a colorful addition to any meadow garden or sunny flower bed. Others, such as common camass and foxglove beardtongue, predominate on the west and east coasts respectively, although they can be found in other areas of Canada where similar soil and climatic conditions prevail. The wildflowers listed below are noted for their hardiness and ability to thrive in garden settings. A separate listing of prairie wildflowers is included in the feature on Backyard Prairies, p. 61.

CROSS-CANADA FAVORITES

✸ BLACK-EYED SUSAN (*Rudbeckia hirta*) — this bright orange-yellow plant grows 12 to 36 inches (30 to 90 cm) tall and blooms from late June through September. Long lasting as a cut flower.

✸ BLAZING STAR (*Liatris spicata*) — 24 to 48 inches (60 to 120 cm) tall, with lavender or pinkish-purple flowers that bloom in July and August. An excellent cut or dried flower.

✸ BUTTERFLY WEED (*Asclepias tuberosa*) — a favorite of butterflies, this 18- to 24-inch (45 to 60 cm) tall plant has orange, yellow or red flowers that bloom from July to September. Makes a good cut flower; seed pods can be dried.

✸ WOOD LILY (*Lilium philadelphicum*) — a 12- to 36-inch (30 to 90 cm) tall species that varies in color from yellow-orange to red-orange and blooms from June to August. Use for accent planting, where its upward-facing blooms will stand out.

✸ CARDINAL FLOWER (*Lobelia cardinalis*) — a spectacular scarlet-red July bloomer, 24 to 42 inches (60 to 105 cm) tall. Likes moist, slightly acidic soil and uncrowded space. Its sweet nectar attracts hummingbirds.

◀ *Black-eyed Susans*

▲ *Blazing Star* Cardinal Flower ▼

❧ OBEDIENT PLANT (*Physostegia virginiana*) — a 24- to 36-inch (60 to 90 cm) plant with lavender to rosy-pink flowers that resemble snapdragons and grow in rows on a square, terminal spike from late June through September. Its common name comes from the flower's tendency to stay put when it is moved to one side of the spike. Spreads by a creeping stolon root that creates large clumps and drifts, and favors well-drained, humus-rich soil.

❧ MOUNTAIN MINT (*Pycnanthemum virginianum*) — a dependable meadow species with a pleasant thyme-like fragrance. Grows 24 inches (60 cm) tall and has small white flowers in compact, flat-topped clusters that bloom in July through September. A good companion plant with asters and goldenrod.

(Top left) Bee Balm; (bottom left) Purple Coneflower; (above) A bouquet of meadow flowers.

❧ NEW ENGLAND ASTER (*Aster novae-angliae*) — ranges in color from deep violet to rosy pink, and is especially effective with goldenrod. Grows 24 to 54 inches (60 to 135 cm) tall and blooms from August to the first frost.

❧ PURPLE CONEFLOWER (*Echinacea purpurea*) — a striking purple flower that grows 30 to 54 inches (75 to 135 cm) tall and blooms from late July to the first frost. Attracts both bees and butterflies. Excellent as a fresh or dried cut flower.

❧ BEE BALM (*Monarda didyma*) — 12 to 36 inches (30 to 90 cm) tall. Bright red blooms in July and August attract butterflies. Wild bergamot (*M. fistulosa*) is similar in growth but has pinkish to pale-lilac flowers.

WEST COAST

❦ BEAR GRASS (*Xerophyllum tenax*) — this striking 24- to 48-inch (60 to 120 cm) tall plant of the upland meadows and rocky slopes has grass-like leaves and unique creamy-white flowers massed together in the shape of an upside-down cone. Striking with lilies, cosmos or compass plants.

❦ GLOBE MALLOW (*Iliamna rivularis*) — a robust perennial that grows 36 to 60 inches (90 to 150 cm) tall. Resembles the hollyhock, with maple-like leaves and pinkish-lavender to rose-purple flowers. Does well in full sun with moderate moisture.

❦ FIREWEED (*Epilobium angustifolium*) — also known as willow herb. Grows 48 to 72 inches (120 to 180 cm) tall, with showy pink to magenta four-petalled blooms covering a flowered spike. A prolific, reliable summer bloomer that self-sows easily. Plant in dry, nutrient-poor soil to help keep it in place. This is the floral emblem of the Yukon. It also grows well on the east coast.

❦ WILD BLUE FLAX (*Linum perenne* var. *lewisii*) — closely related to the European species from which linen is made. Has several 12- to 24-inch (30 to 60 cm) tall stems with numerous greyish leaves and clusters of sky-blue flowers arched to one side. Blooms from late spring to midsummer and prefers full sun and well-drained soil.

(Left and inset) Fireweed; (above) Wild Blue Flax and California Poppies (Eschscholzia californica)

❧ COMMON CAMASS (*Camassia quamash*) — a native of British Columbia and a member of the lily family, with numerous violet blue, star-like flowers on 18- to 24-inch (45 to 60 cm) spikes. Often used for naturalizing in dampish meadows, swales (low-lying or depressed and often-wet stretches of land) and on moist slopes. Prefers moist conditions in winter and early spring only; needs to dry out after flowering in spring.

❧ TIGER LILY (*Lilium columbianum*) — popular with west-coast gardeners, this leafy plant grows 36 to 48 inches (90 to 120 cm) tall and has small orange and spotted red bell-like flowers. Use as an early-summer meadow accent.

❧ BLUE-EYED GRASS (*Sisyrinchium douglasii*) — related to the iris family, this 12- to 18-inch (30 to 45 cm) tall grassy plant has exquisite, six-petalled deep purple to magenta flowers. Prefers wet, open meadows, full sun and nutrient-poor soil.

❧ BLANKETFLOWER (*Gaillardia aristata*) — one of the showiest of meadow wildflowers, this 24- to 48-inch (60 to 120 cm) tall, drought-tolerant perennial from the prairies and British Columbia is a favorite of meadow seed mixes across the country. Yellow and red daisy-like flowers bloom throughout the summer. Requires full sun and well-drained soil. Striking with butterfly weed and wild bergamot.

EAST COAST

❧ FOXGLOVE BEARDTONGUE (*Penstemon digitalis*) — this 24- to 48-inch (60 to 120 cm) tall native resembles foxglove and has white to whitish-pink tubular flowers. It blooms from late May to July in fields, prairies and woodland clearings throughout New Brunswick and Nova Scotia. Tolerates dry, nutrient-poor soil and will appeal to gardeners concerned with water conservation.

❧ EVENING PRIMROSE (*Oenothera biennis*) — a 24- to 48-inch (60 to 120 cm) tall drought-tolerant biennial that is clumped or bushy in appearance, with showy, four-petalled pure yellow flowers that open during cloudy days and sometimes in full sun. Useful along roadsides leading to a cottage or country residence. The long seedheads provide winter food for birds. *O. fruticosa*, commonly called sundrops, blooms in the day.

❧ COMMON ST. JOHN'S WORT (*Hypericum perforatum*) — a bushy plant that grows 24 to 36 inches (60 to 90 cm) tall, with small five-petalled flowers that have black dots around their margins. Although not a native plant, this tough, dependable species has established itself here and thrives in full sun and dry, nutrient-poor soil. It delivers an abundance of color to a meadow. Can be invasive.

❧ PEARLY EVERLASTING (*Anaphalis margaritacea*) — found in most meadows, pastures and roadsides in the Maritimes as well as across the rest of Canada. Clusters of papery white bracts surround the yellow flowerlets of this dense, bushy plant and make it especially suitable for dried-flower arrangements. It grows 24 to 36 inches (60 to 90 cm) tall from a strong root rhizome and persists in drier soils.

❧ COMMON FLEABANE (*Erigeron philadelphicus*) — this 12- to 24-inch (30 to 60 cm) summer meadow plant has dainty white to pinkish-white flowers that form a striking mass effect in groups. A good species for naturalizing in moist meadows. Like most of the daisy family, it is attractive to butterflies and moths.

◀ *Sundrops (bottom right) in a country garden.*

▲ *Pearly Everlasting*

▲ *Common Fleabane*   *Blazing Star* ▼

Lovely
Lupines

After the last of winter's snow has melted and the delicate flowers of spring have completed their life cycle, lupines rise and explode with color, announcing summer's return. In the Maritimes especially, they fill the fields and roadsides like an undulating sea of delightful blue, pink and purple spires.

❧ Lupines belong to the pea family (*Leguminosae*), which includes peashrub, wisteria and yellowwood. The genus, *Lupinus*, includes about 200 species, most of which are perennial and many of which are native to North America.

❧ The plant's name is derived from *lupus*, Latin for wolf, because it was once thought to deplete — or "wolf" — the soil's mineral content. In fact, lupines thrive in poor soil and, like all members of the *Leguminosae* family, they actually enhance soil fertility by fixing atmospheric nitrogen into a useable nutrient.

❧ The lupine's pea-like flowers are arranged in a tight mass around the flower stalk. The various species grow from 12 to 60 inches (30 cm to 1.5 m) tall and have a strong taproot. Although it is not known for its scent, a field of lupines permeates the air with a sweet but tangy pepper fragrance.

Cultivating Lupines

❧ Not all gardens are suited to growing lupines. Lupines thrive along the moist eastern seaboard and other humid climates, but don't do well where summers are hot and dry. They grow best in well-drained, slightly acidic soils. Few wild varieties are adaptable to the garden — the choices are limited to *L. perennis* or the hardy *L. polyphyllus*.

❧ Because they have a taproot system that doesn't recover well from transplanting, start lupines from seed either indoors in late winter or sow directly into the garden in late June.

❧ Wild plants dug up from a field have little chance of gaining a foothold in the garden; however, seed can be gathered in the wild, germinated and planted out as seedlings.

❧ Started plants of lupine hybrids are available in nurseries in the spring, but a wider choice of cultivars is available from seed.

Starting from Seed

❧ Lupine seeds have hard seed coats that need special treatment to soften them so moisture can penetrate and activate the embryos.

❧ Seeds can be either frozen for 48 hours after soaking in a wet paper towel for 24 hours (freezing after soaking improves germination), or filed with a nail file or fine sandpaper to allow moisture to be absorbed.

❧ After soaking, sow seeds in peat pots to avoid disturbing the roots when transplanting. Plant two seeds to each pot, 1/4 inch (6 mm) deep, and keep the soil temperature at about 54°F (12°C). Higher soil temperatures prevent sprouting.

❧ Use light, well-drained sandy soil or a soilless planting mix with a pH of 6.5 to 6.9; lupines like slightly acidic soil.

❧ Seeds germinate irregularly over a 14-day period, depending on the color of the flower. Unusual colors are slower to germinate.

Planting

❧ The area is best prepared the fall before planting. Lupines thrive in a well-drained sandy loam, rich in humus, so work in lots of peat moss or decayed leaves, which also create a slightly acidic soil. Each spring, dust bonemeal lightly around plants to encourage blooming.

❧ Set the seedlings out after hardening off, spacing the plants 24 inches (60 cm) apart. A mulch of grass clippings helps shade the roots and keeps them moist. Plants will bloom the first year and be spectacular the second.

The Growing Season

❧ Lupines grow from April to July, with flowering occurring in June. The flowers last about two to three weeks, if conditions are cool; plants may not bloom at all if conditions are too hot and humid.

❧ To encourage a second bloom, remove spent flowers as they fade.

❧ If you let your flowers go to seed, cut down the flowering stems to ground level in November. A light straw mulch helps winter over the plants.

❧ Lupines, especially the hybrids, aren't long-lived plants and will last only three or four years. Start new plants every couple of years.

WILD LUPINES *from* SEA *to* SEA

❧ The lupines seen in fields and on roadsides in the Maritimes are *Lupinus polyphyllus*, which form large drifts in dry sites and flower in late June and early July. In spite of its proliferation, this is an introduced species native to the Pacific northwest from British Columbia to California that has naturalized and flourished in eastern Canada.

❧ Large drifts of brightly colored lupines are also seen along roadsides north of the Great Lakes in central Canada. They are garden escapees and descendants of Russell hybrids, hardy survivors to Zone 2b.

❧ Travelling farther west, the number of lupine varieties increases dramatically. Tree lupine (*L. arboreus*) isn't a tree, but does form a shrub in British Columbia. A native of California, it was introduced to B.C. to stabilize steep banks. Tree lupine is the source of the yellow color in Russell hybrids.

❧ Probably the most common of the western species is silky lupine (*L. sericeus*), a native that grows from northern B.C. to Arizona. It makes large drifts, especially among yellow pine. Leaves are covered with long hairs that give the plants a silky appearance.

PRAIRIE GARDENS

*A prairie garden captures in miniature the spirit and movement of
vast grasslands, dotted with colorful prairie flowers and teeming with wildlife
of every kind — including butterflies, birds, rabbits and mice.*

Once, the Great Plains of North America were covered with a rippling blanket of wild grasses and flowers. Larkspur, vetches, windflowers, avens, wild roses and scores of other blossoms spangled a grassy ocean that stretched from Winnipeg to the Rocky Mountains. Every year, buffalo, fires and autumn frosts killed off the vegetation and added more biomass to the rich prairie soil. Root fibers protected the soil from erosion by wind and rain. The root systems of perennial native plants and grasses sprouted new life each spring. In this way, the wild prairie thrived undisturbed for thousands of years.

Although modern agriculture has denuded much of the land of hundreds of perennial native species, a concerted effort by concerned biologists and local citizens in recent years has resulted in the establishment of new prairie habitats and the return of native plants to their prairie roots. With a growing awareness of the benefits of using drought-tolerant native plants in commercial and public landscaping, prairie grasses and wildflowers now grow freely along highway roadsides, at public rest areas, in home gardens and on the grounds of shopping centers and other commercial developments.

But how do prairies differ from meadows?

Ironically, "prairie" is the French word for meadow. The early French settlers had no other word to describe the open, grass-covered, treeless landscape they found in what is now the middle of North America. But there is quite a difference between prairies and meadows as we think of them now — and much of that difference lies in the composition of the two areas. If we imagine a meadow, a field of wildflowers is what immediately comes to mind. The grasses are certainly there, but theirs is a supporting role. In a prairie, the reverse is true. Grasses predominate, and we often substitute the word "grasslands" for prairie.

The prairie is a land of extreme variability — hot, dry summers and bitterly cold, dry winters. Annual rainfall can vary from as much as 40 inches (100 cm) in one area to less than 10 inches (25 cm) in another. Prairie plants have survived climatic changes, fire and drought, and today's species are well adapted to harsh conditions. Fire, in fact, is a natural prairie phenomenon — it stimulates the warm-season plants, causing them to send up new growth. It weakens the seeds and plants of cold-season grasses and weeds such as dandelions and thistles, which sprout beneath the snow and get a head start on prairie plants. And it controls new shrubs and tree saplings that, once established, would cast pools of

shade on the sun-loving prairie plants, and change the prairie landscape into arboreal forest.

Depending on the type of soil and amount of moisture, a prairie can vary greatly and each plant species has individual preferences for soil type, moisture and a variety of other factors. Prairie grasses and plants parade their floral colors across the landscape from the first prairie willow of April to the last bottle gentian of late September. About 17 different species come into flower each week, bloom for a short time, and move on to seed production. This rapid succession reduces competition and gives each plant its time and place in the sun. It also brings many different kinds of insect life to the prairie garden all summer long.

Growing *your own* Backyard Prairie

Like all other natural gardens, native prairie gardens are environmentally friendly. Because most of the plants are perennials with deep root systems, they're ideal for soil conservation; bees, butterflies and birds love them; and, once established, a prairie garden is virtually maintenance-free, requiring next to nothing in the way of insecticides, herbicides and fertilizers. Most important, the plants have evolved locally and can withstand the frigid winters and scorching summers of a prairie habitat, as well as prolonged periods of little rain. Although they're perfectly adaptable to urban spaces, native prairie gardens bear little resemblance to the typical city garden.

A sea of grasses, studded with constantly changing wildflowers, provides an undulating landscape of color and texture from early spring into October. With their muted shades of green, gold or brown, their soft textures and their striking seedheads, grasses are the dramatic foil for the prairie flowers that appear throughout the year — April brings the prairie crocus; June, the cutleaf anemone; summer, the radiant blazing star, gaillardia and fireweed; and autumn, purple asters, goldenrod, and fringed and bottle gentians.

Preparing *the* Site

Site preparation the year before sowing even one seed is crucial (see Meadow Gardens, p. 44). Native plants may withstand drought, frost and wind, but they're no match for a host of non-native weeds. Perennial species such as quack grass, brome grass, the cultivated Kentucky bluegrass, dandelion and Canada thistle are the most likely to create competition. Annual weeds give less trouble because most prairie plants can outcompete them by the second or third year.

❦ Start in the spring by weeding the area you've chosen for your garden, making sure to remove the entire root system of each plant. Spot applications of an approved herbicide may be necessary to eradicate stubborn weeds. Control newly germinated weeds as recommended in the section on Meadow Gardens (p. 45). Do not use a power tiller, as this brings too much fresh soil, rich in weed seed, to the surface.

Sowing *and* Maintenance

❦ The soil should be firmed well before planting the following spring; a lawn roller will do the job. Late spring or early summer is the best time to seed, since most prairie wildflowers and grasses are warm-season plants which germinate best after soil temperatures have warmed up.

❦ A prairie garden takes time to establish itself, from three to five years from seed. Seedlings don't show much growth the first year, preferring to put down good roots. Be patient and keep weeding the plot into the second season; by the third, your efforts will pay off.

❦ Once a prairie garden is established, it will need to be mowed or burned every few years to remove weeds and dead material and to provide nutrients for the soil — either as mulch, if mown, or as beneficial ash, if burned. Make sure you obtain the permission and cooperation of the local fire department before burning.

Prairie Plants *for your* Garden

GRASSES

❧ BIG BLUESTEM (*Andropogon gerardii*) — shoulder-high, reddish-mauve stalks, 36 inches to 8 feet (90 cm to 240 cm) tall, with a three-pronged seed head that resembles a turkey's foot. This is the grass that nourished the buffalo on the early prairie. Stems and leaves turn from green to reddish-copper with the first frost. Long-lived and showy, it holds its color well when dried. Can be used in both meadow and prairie plantings.

❧ LITTLE BLUESTEM (*Andropogon scoparius*) — shorter and more delicate than big bluestem, this 24- to 36-inch (60 to 90 cm) grass has downy, translucent seedheads. Bottom shoots are bluish and leaf blades tend to fold. Good for dry areas and wildlife gardens.

❧ INDIAN GRASS (*Sorghastrum nutans*) — graceful bronze seedheads on 48- to 84-inch (120 to 240 cm) stalks; one of the most showy late-season plants. Both seedheads and flower clusters are filled with short, golden-brown hairs. Good with big bluestem.

❧ PRAIRIE DROPSEED (*Sporobolus heterolepis*) — Fragrant, with long, narrow leaf blades and edible seeds. One of the most beautiful of the native grasses, it grows 24 to 36 inches (60 to 90 cm) tall and resembles fountain grass.

❧ JUNE GRASS (*Koeleria cristata*) — a short, 12- to 24-inch (30 to 60 cm) species, drought tolerant, with showy, open, shiny white seedheads in June. Likes rocky soil and sunny spots. A good companion to pasqueflower and prairie smoke.

❧ NEEDLE GRASS (*Stipa comata*) — delicate and graceful, with a curly, plumed seedhead. Grows 24 to 36 inches (60 to 90 cm) tall and tolerates very dry sites.

Big Bluestem

Indian Grass

PRAIRIE WILDFLOWERS

❧ WHITE CAMASS (*Zigadenus elegans*) — a member of the lily family, with a cluster of greenish-white flowers on 12- to 24-inch (30 to 60 cm) stalks. Blooms before most summer flowers and grasses have begun to grow.

❧ CANADA MILKVETCH (*Astragalus canadensis*) — densely branched stems with large pagoda-like spikes of fragrant creamy-yellow blossoms from July to the end of August. Plants grow to 48 inches (120 cm) and are popular with butterflies and bees. Resembles lupine and is an aggressive, spreading species.

❧ YELLOW CONEFLOWER (*Ratbida columnifera*) — an unusual wildflower with reflexing yellow petals and a prominent cone. Grows up to 24 inches (60 cm) tall and blooms from June to September.

❧ PALE-SPIKE LOBELIA (*Lobelia spicata*) — delicate blue to white trumpet-shape flowers on 12-inch (30 cm) plants. Blooms from late June to August.

❧ PURPLE PRAIRIE CLOVER (*Petalostemum purpureum*) — with attractive purple conical flowers that bloom in July and August, this legume is striking with bush clover, flowering spurge and blazing star. Grows 12 to 36 inches (30 to 90 cm) tall and does well in dry, sandy soil.

❧ PRAIRIE YELLOW VIOLET (*Viola nuttallii*) — a dainty, 6-inch (15 cm) plant with lance-shape basal leaves and pretty yellow flowers, touched with brown, that bloom from late April through May.

❧ VEINY MEADOWRUE (*Thalictrum venulosum*) — dense clusters of white flowers on long stalks. Often found in woodlands because it is shade-tolerant. Grows 60 inches (1.5 m) tall.

❧ NODDING PINK ONION (*Allium cernuum*) — an easy-to-grow prairie bulb that reaches 12 to 24 inches (30 to 60 cm). Attractive nodding, globe-like flowers bloom in July and August. Prefers slightly moist soil and will form substantial clumps from bulb offsets.

Purple Prairie Clover

Yellow Coneflower

Prairie Smoke

❧ BLUE BOTTLE GENTIAN OR CLOSED GENTIAN (*Gentiana andrewsii*) — an erect plant, 12 to 24 inches (30 to 60 cm) tall, with striking deep blue, closed flowers that bloom from late August through the fall and resemble little bottles. It favors wet prairies, and is particularly effective paired with asters and goldenrod.

❧ GIANT HYSSOP (*Agastache foeniculum*) — a member of the mint family, this 40-inch (1 m) tall plant has spikes of lavender blooms that are alive with bees and butterflies from June to September.

❧ DOTTED BLAZING STAR (*Liatris punctata*) — a small, feathery 24-inch (60 cm) plant with numerous spikes of purple flowers that open from the bottom to the top and bloom mid- to late summer.

❧ STIFF GOLDENROD (*Solidago rigida*) — a stiff and erect 24- to 48-inch (60 to 120 cm) plant with beautiful, flat-topped yellow flowers that light up a prairie or meadow garden from August to October. Provides fall color, especially in combination with big bluestem, prairie clover and leadplant, and attracts butterflies.

❧ CULVER'S ROOT (*Veronicastrum virginicum*) — a spectacular tall-grass prairie plant with slender spikes of white flowers. Grows 36 to 60 inches (90 to 150 cm) tall and blooms mid- to late summer. Likes medium to moist, rich soil.

❧ PRAIRIE SMOKE (*Geum triflorum*) — an 8- to 12-inch (20 to 30 cm) plant with dull red sepals and pink flowers in May and early June. Spectacular seedheads, with long, feathery pink hairs attached to the maturing seed, resemble puffs of smoke. This species is drought tolerant and does well in infertile, sandy soil. In a non-prairie garden, it can be be used in rockeries, as a ground cover in full sun or at the front of a perennial flowerbed.

❧ HAIRY PUCCOON (*Lithospermum croceum*) — this dainty, 8- to 12-inch (20 to 30 cm) plant has lovely golden-yellow tube-shape flowers in a flat, bent cluster. Individual flowers resemble forget-me-nots. The stems and leaves are covered with dense, white downy hairs (hence its common name). It tolerates dry soils and is used in prairie restorations and in combination with other low to mid-height prairie natives.

❧ PRAIRIE CROCUS OR PASQUEFLOWER (*Pulsatilla patens or Anemone patens*) — furry-stemmed yellow or mauve blooms hug the ground in the snow and announce the arrival of spring. It likes dry, sandy or gravelly soil in lots of sun and is Manitoba's floral emblem.

▲ *Hairy Puccoon*

▲ *Culver's Root*   *Prairie Crocus* ▼

Northern Sea Oat

Silver or Eulalie Grass

Golden Foxtail

Ornamental Grasses

Ornamental grasses are one of the rediscovered treasures of modern gardens. They act as a foil for more showy perennials, and their gently arching form adds contrast to the stiffness of other plants. Many grasses come into their own in late fall and early winter when their plumes or seeds add beauty to an otherwise barren landscape.

As a group, grasses are very versatile plants. Species can be chosen to grow in almost any location — from open, dry meadow to moist woodland. In the natural garden, they are valuable both as butterfly larvae food and as a seed source for wintering birds. Because they are relatively new to the Canadian gardening scene, their hardiness is not fully known. The zone ratings given here are probably conservative and some species could well survive much colder climates than indicated.

❦ GARDENER'S GARTERS (*Phalaris arundinacea*) — a somewhat invasive grass, useful for stabilizing slopes. The green and white striped foliage is the main attraction. Will grow well in dry or moist soils. Zone 4.

❦ GOLDEN FOXTAIL (*Alopecurus pratensis aureus*) — pale brown flower heads in early summer on 24-inch (60 cm) stems above the yellow foliage. Zone 5.

❦ SILVER OR EULALIE GRASS (*Miscanthus sinensis*) — a robust, clump-forming grass that will grow up to 72 inches (1.8 m) tall, depending on the variety. Grown primarily for the showy seedheads produced in late summer. 'Blue Wonder' has a bluish sheen, 'Morning Light' is more silvery. The variegated form has leaves striped in yellow and green, and the Japanese is a dwarf form. Zone 5b.

❦ NORTHERN SEA OAT (*Chasmanthium latifolium*) — will grow equally well in shade or full sun. The arching seedheads, on 36- to 60-inch (90 to 150 cm) stems, turn a rusty brown in fall and persist into winter. A good specimen plant. Zone 4.

Fountain Grass

Japanese Blood Grass

Gardener's Garters

❧ FOUNTAIN GRASS (*Pennisetum setaceum*) — upright, arching stems form a large clump in a few years. It can be grown from seed where it is not hardy and treated as an annual. The showy plumes of feathery seed on stems up to 48 inches (120 cm) tall are attractive from late summer onward. Zone 7.

❧ UPRIGHT SEDGE (*Carex conica marginata*) — a dwarf clump-forming sedge that reaches 4 inches (10 cm) and will take quite dry conditions. Zone 5b.

❧ JAPANESE BLOOD GRASS (*Imperata* 'Red Baron') — a low spreading grass, up to 12 inches (30 cm) tall, that is grown chiefly for its bright red stems; the seedheads are not showy. Grows best in light shade and makes an impressive clump when mature. Zone 5.

❧ BRONZE TUFTED HAIRGRASS (*Deschampsia caespitosa*) — forms a dark green mound up to 24 inches (60 cm) high with feathery flower spikes in late summer that last well for winter effect. Zone 5.

❧ JOB'S TEARS (*Coix lachryma*) — short-lived but will self-seed. Forms a loose clump, up to 48 inches (120 cm) tall, with pale green foliage and attractive seedheads. A good specimen plant. Zone 5.

❧ SKINNER'S GOLDEN BROME (*Bromus inermis* 'Skinner's Golden') — yellow-striped foliage and feathery flower stems. Grows to 36 inches (90 cm). Zone 1.

❧ BLUE OAT GRASS (*Helictotrichon sempervirens*) — a shorter, mound-forming clump grass growing around 24 inches (60 cm) tall. The leaves are a greyish-blue and turn brown in winter but remain interesting. Flowers and seedheads are not very showy. Zone 4.

❧ GOLDEN MILLET (*Millium effusum*) — a tufted, clump-forming plant which spreads slowly by underground runners. Grows best in moist locations and light, dappled shade. The plants grow about 24 inches (60 cm) tall, with the flowers growing another 12 inches (30 cm). Zone 5.

WILDLIFE
in the
GARDEN

*A garden that is
fully attuned to nature is alive with the sound and
movement of wildlife. Within its boundaries,
birds, butterflies and other animals co-exist —
finding food, shelter, water and living space in a setting
inspired by nature and designed by man.*

U nlike an ornamental garden, which is prized for its beauty alone, a natural garden not only delights the eye but also offers a habitat for many kinds of wildlife. Birds such as woodpeckers, cardinals, chickadees and hummingbirds come daily to feast on insects, berries or nectar, while butterflies and bees flit from one brightly colored flower to another and frogs sun themselves on lush green lily pads.

The wildlife you attract to your garden depends, in large measure, on what you plant there. To encourage visits from colorful and beneficial species, you will need to provide the food, shelter and living space they require. If you are interested in particular birds, for example, you should research their food and nesting requirements. A nature store or wildlife association can provide information; observing birds or butterflies in their natural habitat is also a good place to start.

Except during periods of drought, it is not essential to supply water for garden wildlife, since it can be taken from rain puddles, dew or garden ponds. In winter, however, water is scarce — and it's crucial to the survival of birds. An aquarium heater installed in a birdbath will keep it free of ice during cold weather. Be sure any birdbath, pool or other source of water for birds is located in an open area and near bushes or shrubs so that birds can spot, and escape from, predator cats.

Natural — by Design

A lthough nature itself is your best cue to creating a natural-looking wildlife habitat in a garden setting, here are some guidelines to follow.

❧ To offer protection, food and nesting sites, plant trees, shrubs, flowers and grass to recreate the layered effect found in nature.

❧ Since wildlife tends to be more abundant along the boundaries, or edges, between plant communities, the more edge you create in your garden, the more wildlife you'll attract. Make the edges sinuous and informal, with grass tapering gradually to wildflowers, then to shrubs and trees. Robins, for example, thrive at ground level, while goldfinches and cardinals prefer shrubs, and tanagers and orioles seek the upper canopy of tall trees.

❧ To attract the greatest range of animal life, plant trees, shrubs, vines and flowers from as many different species as possible.

❧ Arrange plants in groves or clumps, as they grow naturally. Plant large shrubs and small trees more densely than is usually recommended; they provide good cover and also make a striking impression. Plant shrub borders at least 6 feet (2 m) deep. Many birds nest quite close to the ground and prefer well-protected sites. The deeper and denser the shrub cover, the more likely it will be used for nesting.

From water in a birdbath to the seeds and nectar of native plants, a natural garden provides nourishment for many kinds of wildlife.

❧ Include evergreens, which offer shelter and attractive green foliage year-round.

❧ Introduce natural elements such as water, rocks and tree stumps to provide nesting opportunities and shelter for many insects and small animals.

❧ Leave the stalks of perennials in your garden until spring so that wintering wildlife have valuable cover and a source of food. The leaves and stalks also provide an overwintering site for many insects and help trap snow, which adds a layer of insulation for those hibernating in the soil.

❧ Include herbaceous plants from the daisy family — such as sunflowers, thistles, goldenrod, black-eyed Susan and coreopsis — which offer the most abundant and sought-after seed crop for birds and are also a good food source for butterflies and many other insects.

❧ Plant for a succession of blooms from spring to fall to ensure a continuous food supply for hummingbirds, bees and butterflies.

❧ Don't remove leaves or clippings in the garden. They provide shelter for beneficial insects such as centipedes and beetles that keep other insect species in balance — and plant debris also returns nutrients to the soil as it decays.

❧ Don't use broad-spectrum insecticide sprays. Flowering plants depend on the many insects that feed on their nectar for pollination, and pollinated plants produce more abundant flowers and seeds. Insecticides also deplete the insect population on which birds rely. If essential, lethal pest attacks can be controlled using a biodegradable insecticide with low persistence, such as insecticidal soap.

Birds *in the* Garden

Birds are welcome guests in a natural garden. Their color, song and patterns of flight are reason enough to delight us, but they also provide one of nature's best methods of insect control. During the summer, omnivorous birds eat many times their weight in grubs and mosquitoes, along with a steady diet of seeds and berries. However, once the insect population dies or goes into hibernation in the autumn, these birds need an alternative source of the proteins and lipids that insects normally supply to their diet — and seeds and fruit fit the bill. A source of fall and winter food is also crucial to birds that live on plants all year.

Since birds must maintain a constant body temperature throughout the winter in order to survive, they depend on heat- and energy-producing food — especially in late winter, when most of their food sources have been depleted. Any plant that produces a large

Berries of all kinds, especially ones that stay on trees late in the season, are a vital source of heat- and energy-producing food for birds in winter.

quantity of seeds or fleshy fruit is a boon to the natural garden, especially if the seeds stay attached well into the winter or following spring. Many of the tart and less desirable berries, such as highbush cranberry (*Viburnum trilobum*), are left untouched by birds in late summer and through the autumn and become life-saving food in late winter. Successive freeze and thaw cycles concentrate the sugar content of the fruit and make it an appealing food source for the hungry birds long after the sweet berries of summer have been picked from the trees.

Protection from predators and from the severe conditions of winter are also essential in nurturing a bird population. Trees and shrubs with dense foliage provide summer shelter; evergreens or thorny deciduous plants, such as hawthorn, offer protection in every season and also make ideal nesting sites, especially if there are spreading horizontal branches to give support. When planting evergreens, cluster them toward the corners or along the sides of the lot to create a windbreak and a natural screen, positioning other food plants nearby.

Habitats *for* Birds

TREES

❧ Of all woody plants in North America, pines are considered the most important to songbirds. Red pine (*Pinus resinosa*) is handsome, rapid-growing, hardy and generally resistant to diseases. Eastern white pine (*P. strobus*), one of the most beautiful native pines, is particularly useful as a background for flowering trees and shrubs. White pine attracts woodpeckers, waxwings, warblers, chickadees and grosbeaks. Owls roost in pines during the day and the horizontal branches provide platform-like nesting sites for robins, blue jays and mourning doves. Coniferous trees also provide valuable shelter for roosting birds during cold winter nights.

❧ The dense foliage of white cedar (*Thuja occidentalis*) makes an excellent hedge and provides effective shelter for birds when planted in groups of three or more. The seeds are eaten by pine siskins, crossbills and redpolls. Chickadees shelter in white cedar and feed on egg masses of pests like tent caterpillar and gypsy moth.

❧ Yews (*Taxus canadensis* and *T. cuspidata*) provide a fine, dark green ornamental background for other plants and offer good winter cover for birds. Because yews tolerate shade, they're especially useful in foundation plantings on the north side of buildings. Mockingbirds, robins, and chipping and song sparrows nest in them and eat the attractive red fruits. A word of warning — the seeds inside yew fruits are very poisonous to humans.

Trees, shrubs, flowers and grass that are planted to recreate the layered effect found in nature offer the best protection, food and nesting sites for birds in a garden setting.

❧ Among deciduous trees, birches attract juncos, chickadees and nuthatches, while oaks are preferred by blue jays. Hawthorns provide berries and nesting sites for almost 30 species of birds. Many songbirds, such as cardinals and robins, favor flowering dogwoods, pin cherries and serviceberries.

Staghorn Sumac (Rhus typhina)

SHRUBS

❧ In natural settings, staghorn sumac (*Rhus typhina*) establishes itself well on dry, sunny sites. It adapts easily to gardens where its interesting foliage and crimson autumn color can be used to striking effect. The cone-shape fruit clusters contain seeds with a high oil content and persist well into late winter, much to the delight of more than 50 species of birds, including cardinals, blue jays and evening grosbeaks.

❧ Migrating thrushes, robins, catbirds and brown thrashers relish the fruits of honeysuckle (*Lonicera* spp.) in late October when few other succulent fruits are available. Most species are hardy, and adaptable to poor soils and cold winter temperatures.

❧ In the dead of winter, the brilliant red branches of red-osier dogwood (*Cornus sericea*) bring a welcome splash of color to an otherwise bleak landscape. This plant tolerates the same wet sites that willows occupy. Thickets make attractive nest sites for red-winged blackbirds and yellow warblers, while the shrubs' abundant white fruits provide food for more than 100 species of song and game birds. The grey dogwood (*C. racemosa*) grows equally well in moist or dry soils, in sun or in shade. Highly suited to the urban landscape, it tolerates air pollution as well as severe pruning and offers a dense cover for birds. Its ornamental white berries are eaten in summer and autumn.

❧ Winterberry (*Ilex verticillata*), a native deciduous holly, provides fruit for winter bird species. Inkberry (*I. glabra*), on the other hand, while not as hardy, is evergreen and thus offers both food and winter cover.

CLIMBERS AND GROUND COVERS

❧ Wintergreen (*Gaultheria procumbens*), bearberry (*Arctostaphylos uva-ursi*), partridgeberry (*Mitchella repens*), bunchberry (*Cornus canadensis*) and wild strawberry (*Fragaria virginiana*) are all native ground covers with edible red fruits that appeal to birds.

❧ One of the best vines for birds is bittersweet (*Celastrus scandens*). It grows to 25 feet (8 m) if given room on an arbor or trellis. Three to five plants, both male and female, provide an adequate crop of berries that blue birds and robins enjoy.

❧ Virginia creeper (*Parthenocissus quinquefolia*) and wild riverbank grape (*Vitis riparia*) are both an unbeatable lure for birds. The attractive five-lobed leaves of Virginia creeper turn scarlet in the fall, heralding a bounty of dark-blue berries that last into the winter — a feast for many species, including red-headed woodpeckers.

❧ Brambles of any kind (raspberries, blackberries and roses), with their sharp thorns, afford birds reliable protection from predators. Their natural habitat is old fields, hedgerows and clearings where they form dense tangles. The soft black or red fruits and the vitamin C-rich hips are eaten by many birds. Hips may also persist into winter and provide essential food for overwintering birds.

❧ Cotoneasters (*Cotoneaster microphyllus* and *C. apiculatus*) are shiny-leafed low evergreens, particularly effective in rock gardens or on embankments. The red fruits remain on plants through the winter and provide a valuable food source for purple finches, blue jays, doves, evening grosbeaks and partridges.

(Clockwise from far left)
The dark-blue berries
and scarlet autumn foliage
of Virginia creeper;
winterberry, edged by white
alyssum; wild riverbank
grape, with its plump purple
fruit; wild strawberries.

ANNUALS AND PERENNIALS

In addition to woody plants, many annuals and perennials produce abundant seeds valuable to bird species that feed on or near the ground.

❧ If you want seeds on your plants, don't deadhead the flowers; they need to die on the plant in order to produce seeds. A word of caution, though — many modern cultivars found in nurseries and garden centers are sterile hybrids that produce beautiful showy flowers, but no seeds. When selecting asters, zinnias, petunias and marigolds in particular, choose open-pollinated, old-fashioned species.

Flowers from the daisy family, including thistles and sunflowers, provide the most sought-after seeds for birds.

❧ When planting flowers to attract wildlife, choose native specimens first since these have been a longstanding natural food source for wildlife in the area. Other good annuals and perennials include love-lies-bleeding (*Amaranthus*), cornflower (*Centaurea cyanus*), pot marigold (*Calendula*), bellflower (*Campanula*), chrysanthemums, columbine (*Aquilegia*), coneflowers (*Rudbeckia*), tickseed (*Coreopsis*), cosmos, pinks (*Dianthus*), forget-me-nots (*Myosotis*), four-o'clocks (*Mirabilis*), blanket flower (*Gaillardia*), hollyhocks (*Alcea*), larkspur (*Consolida*), moss rose (*Portulaca*), phlox, sunflowers (*Helianthus*) and vervain (*Verbena*).

Hummingbirds

Delicate, fearless and lightning-quick, hummingbirds have charmed and amazed people for centuries with their dizzying speed and patterns of flight. But this tiny bird that has admiringly been called "a glittering fragment of the rainbow" is a useful garden guest as well. Pollen brushes onto the hummingbird's body and is distributed throughout the garden as the bird darts from flower to flower on its search for food. Hummingbirds also eat a surprising number of insects; some they snatch in mid-air, and others are consumed while feeding at blossoms.

Flying up, down, backward and even upside down, hummingbirds feed every 10 to 15 minutes from dawn to sunset, consuming more than half their weight in food. If you fill a garden with nectar-rich plants that bloom all summer, you'll encourage your tiny visitors to return.

CANADA'S HUMMINGBIRDS

The hummingbird family is large (there are more than 300 species), but most are found in the tropics. Canada's hummingbirds migrate south for the winter and return to their northern breeding grounds in spring. Ruby-throated hummingbirds are found throughout Canada. The male has a bright metallic-red throat; the female's is white with dark spots. Both have green backs and whitish undersides. Considering they're only 3 inches (8 cm) long, the fact that they travel as far south as Texas, Mexico and Costa Rica for the winter is remarkable.

❧ Gardens in western Canada are treated to as many as 14 different species — the rufous, black-chinned and calliope species are the most common. The calliope is also the smallest hummingbird found in Canada; its average weight is 1/10 of an ounce (3 g). The male is iridescent green with long, narrow, purple feathers extending down the sides of its throat. The female has a green back, white breast and dark specks on its throat.

THE RIGHT FLOWERS

The ideal hummingbird plant has red, orange, yellow or pink blooms and either large, solitary flowers or loosely clustered blossoms that often droop. The flowers hold copious reservoirs of nectar at the base of a long, stout floral tube and frequently have protruding stamens or pistils. Scent is unimportant, since hummers depend on sight rather than smell.

❧ Providing layered vegetation is an excellent way to attract hummingbirds. Train a trumpet vine (*Campsis radicans*) or one of the climbing honeysuckles (such as *Lonicera* X *brownii* 'Dropmore Scarlet') on a trellis secured to a fence or wall. Plant a variety of nectar-rich shrubs, like lilac (*Syringa*) and privet (*Ligustrum*), nearby, adding bright-colored annuals and native perennials such as penstemon and cardinal flower (*Lobelia cardinalis*) at their base. Arrange flowers of one color in clumps or similar species together to make a more conspicuous display.

❧ Choose native species where possible and plant so that bloom times overlap, ensuring a steady supply of nectar-producing flowers from early summer until the first frost.

❧ Hummingbirds are territorial; the dominant male may drive others away by defending what he perceives to be his turf. Several plantings, not necessarily within sight of each other, encourage a number of birds without letting any one bird get the upper hand.

NECTAR-RICH PLANTS *for* HUMMINGBIRDS

FLOWERS

A number of the following flowers are also well suited to hanging baskets which you can position near a deck or patio for a close-up look at these delightful garden visitors.

❧ Bee balm
   (*Monarda didyma*)
❧ Bleeding heart
   (*Dicentra spectabilis*)
❧ Butterfly weed
   (*Asclepias tuberosa*)
❧ Canna
❧ Cardinal flower
   (*Lobelia cardinalis*)
❧ Catmint
   (*Nepeta*)
❧ Columbine
   (*Aquilegia*)
❧ Coral bells
   (*Heuchera sanguinea*)
❧ Dahlia
   (*Dahlia merckii*)
❧ Deadnettle
   (*Lamium*)
❧ Delphinium
❧ Flowering tobacco
   (*Nicotiana*)

THE RIGHT FEEDERS

To supplement the blossoms in your garden, especially if spring arrives late and the hummingbirds have already migrated from the south, use a homemade or store-bought feeder that holds a sugar-water solution — it may even be crucial to the hummingbirds' survival. While they like the taste of the sweet solution, a feeder alone is dangerous for the tiny birds because it doesn't provide enough nourishment; a steady diet of sugar water may also cause a fungus in their mouth.

❧ To prepare the sugar-water solution, mix granulated sugar and water in equal proportions; boil to retard fermentation and dissolve the sugar. Dilute to one part boiled sugar mixture to four parts water by adding cold water. Store unused solution in the refrigerator for up to a week. Once hummingbirds have located the feeders, cut the solution back to one part sugar mixture to six parts water. This minimizes the risk of liver damage and encourages the birds to seek more natural foods. To attract hummingbirds to new feeders, paint the feeding tube with red enamel or mount red plastic flowers over the feeder entrance.

❧ Feeders placed too close to windows may invite crashes and disaster; hummingbirds have been unofficially clocked at 30 miles (48 km) per hour, a lightning speed that helps them escape predators. Try hanging a feeder near plants that attract hummingbirds. The tiny birds have remarkable memories and often return to the same feeding sites year after year. Make sure there are trees or shrubs nearby to provide perches for rest breaks.

❧ Although the railing of a deck may seem like a desirable location for hanging a feeder, since it affords easy access to the feeder and brings the hummers close at hand for easy view, bees and wasps will also be attracted to the sugar solution — and may spoil the quiet enjoyment of your deck.

❧ Feeder cleanliness is of the utmost importance. At least once a week, discard any remaining solution, then wash the feeder thoroughly and sterilize with a weak bleach solution. Rinse again thoroughly, and refill with a new supply of sugared water.

❧ Four-o'clock
  (*Mirabilis*)
❧ Foxglove (above)
  (*Digitalis purpurea*)
❧ Fuchsia
  (*Fuchsia hybrida*)
❧ Gladiolus
❧ Hollyhock
  (*Alcea rosea*)
❧ Jewelweed
  (*Impatiens capensis*)
❧ Nasturtium
  (*Tropaeolum majus*)
❧ Penstemon
❧ Petunia (far left)

❧ Phlox
❧ Scarlet sage
  (*Salvia splendens* and
  S. coccinea)
❧ Snapdragon
  (*Antirrhinum majus*)
❧ Spider flower
  (*Cleome spinosa*)
❧ Sweet William
  (*Dianthus barbatus*)
❧ Tulip (red cultivars)
❧ Turtlehead
  (*Chelone*)
❧ Virginia bluebells
  (*Mertensia*)
❧ Zinnia

VINES

❧ Clematis
❧ Climbing honeysuckle
  (*Lonicera*)
❧ Morning-glory
  (*Ipomoea coccinea*
  and *I .purpurea*)
❧ Scarlet runner bean
  (*Phaseolus coccineus*)
❧ Trumpet vine
  (*Campsis radicans*)

SHRUBS

Hummingbirds also visit a number of shrubs and trees searching for insects.

❧ Azalea
❧ Beautybush
  (*Kolkwitzia amabilis*)
❧ Butterfly bush
  (*Buddleia davidii*)
❧ Flowering currant
  (*Ribes aureum*)

❧ Japanese flowering quince
  (*Chaenomeles japonica*)
❧ Lilac
  (*Syringa*)
❧ Privet
  (*Ligustrum*)
❧ Rose of Sharon
  (*Hibiscus syriacus*)
❧ Spirea
❧ Weigela

TREES

❧ Bottlebrush buckeye
  (*Aesculus parviflora*)
❧ Flowering crab apple
  (*Malus*)
❧ Hawthorn
  (*Crataegus*)
❧ Horse chestnut
  (*Aesculus hippocastanum*)
❧ Siberian pea shrub
  (*Caragana arborescens*)
❧ Tulip tree
  (*Liriodendron tulipifera*)

FROGS *and* TOADS *in the* GARDEN

Almost as soon as you install a pond in your garden, frogs will come to visit. The visit may be fleeting or permanent, but welcome in either case.

❧ While most frogs live in or close to water, some, like the leopard frog, will visit a meadow or prairie habitat looking for beetles, grasshoppers and spiders to eat.

❧ Tiny tree frogs eat flies and other small flying insects, and help keep down mosquito larvae in open pools

— but they are seldom seen. You know they are there by the noise they make in spring with their mating calls, and by the frog spawn that fills our pools.

❧ You do not need a pond to have toads in your garden. Toads are ugly, warty and shy, but they are also survivors that live in difficult surroundings and thrive in a natural garden. Toads can breed in small, temporary puddles that would not be suitable for frogs, and their young tadpoles mature much faster than those of frogs.

❧ Although gardeners tolerate toads

at best, toads are much more beneficial in a garden than frogs. They eat flies, slugs, snails, beetles, cutworms, sow bugs and many other pests of man and plant.

❧ While toads rarely live in water, they do like a shallow dishful where they can soak for a few minutes to absorb moisture through their skin, and a cool place where they can wait out the heat of the day. Set out a few water-filled dishes and you will find that your toad population grows and your garden pests disappear.

❧ The one drawback of toads is their habit of burrowing in the soil

Insects *in the* Natural Garden

In addition to the showy butterflies and moths that everyone loves, there are several hundred other species of insects living in your garden. These range in size from tiny flies to large beetles and the majority are essential to the well-being of your soil and plants.

❧ Approximately 99 percent of the insects in your garden are not harmful, and many are actually beneficial. Only a few will feed on plants and people but, unfortunately, these are the ones we notice most.

❧ Some insects copy the warning colors of other insects. Hoverflies, for example, look like tiny wasps and, even though they don't sting, birds will not eat them. Some hoverflies lay their eggs in aphid colonies and contribute a natural control.

❧ Other wasp look-alikes are the insects known as parasitic wasps, which lay their eggs in the host insect (often aphids or caterpillars) and kill them from within. These wasps vary greatly in size from pin-head to almost 1 inch (2.5 cm) long.

❧ Ground beetles, the large, shiny black beetles often found hiding under rocks or boards by day, are

night hunters that feed on cutworms, snail and slug eggs and even climb into trees after tent caterpillars.

❧ The appetite of lady beetles for aphids is well known. It's just a pity their larvae are so strange-looking, like small purple dragons, that many people don't recognize them for the friends they are.

❧ Dragonflies and damselflies range far from their watery homes and grab mosquitoes, midges and no-see-ems as they dart around the garden. A small pond or wet area will encourage them to stay.

❧ While not classified as insects, spiders and mites are some of the most ferocious feeders. Mites tend to be fairly specific in their prey and feed on a limited range of hosts while spiders will eat almost anything smaller than they are — including their mates.

❧ One final friend to watch for is the centipede. These feed on a wide range of other animals in the soil, including millipedes, slugs, small snails and several grubs. They are easy to tell from millipedes by their rapid movement; millipedes tend to curl up into a spring when disturbed.

to hibernate. In a regular garden, there is a constant danger of harming a toad while digging in the fall; in a natural garden, such chores are limited and the danger minimal.

❧ To encourage both frogs and toads, make sure your pond has at least one area where the sides slope gently into the water. Baby tadpoles need to be able to crawl out of the water as they change into adult form — and even frogs cannot swim forever, and need an exit to rest or hunt for food.

Gardens *for* Butterflies

With their brilliant wing patterns and graceful flight, butterflies have long been cherished as symbols of peace and tranquility. Like beautiful flying flowers, they enliven our gardens with color, grace and movement. As they flutter about in search of nectar, they also pollinate many of the flowers they visit (they are second only to bees in this respect) and ensure a seed crop for the following year. Butterflies are also very complex creatures and are highly attuned to their surroundings. Since the larvae often depend on a single plant as a source of food, biologists have begun to use butterflies as a vital indicator of the state of our environment.

Butterflies live two lives, as crawling beast and flying beauty, and each demands a different source of food. If you want to attract — and keep — butterflies in your garden, you'll need to provide a continuous supply of food for both the larva, or caterpillar, and for the adult butterfly.

Since different species seek out different flowers, it's important to learn as much as you can about butterflies so you can select the appropriate plants to meet their needs. By knowing which flowers attract which butterflies, you can design a garden that will ensure your yard is on the flight path of butterflies from spring to the last blooms of fall.

Butterflies are sun-loving insects and their natural habitat is usually a sun-drenched meadow where a range of flowers grow in large numbers. By duplicating the conditions of a meadow in your garden and including native meadow wildflowers, you'll provide butterflies with an abundance of their preferred source of food.

Although butterflies are attracted to most flowers, each species has its preferences. Scent is a powerful magnet and so is flower color — purple shades top the list, followed closely by blue, yellow, pink and white. Most butterflies ignore red flowers unless they're quite fragrant. To attract the attention of passing butterflies, be sure to plant flowers in masses large enough to be noticed from the air.

Lupines (above), black-eyed Susans and purple coneflowers (both left) are favorites of nectar-seeking butterflies.

An old-world swallowtail perches on a purple coneflower.

is a must. Sidewalks or gravel paths provide warm, bright resting places. Walls or hedges around the garden also provide warm and sheltered spots, and ensure vital protection from wind.

❧ Since butterflies can't drink from open water, they like mud puddles and the wet edges of ponds. You can create a butterfly bath in your garden by sinking a bucket of sand into the earth and keeping it wet. Be sure to add a couple of flat rocks as perches.

From Butterfly *to* Caterpillar

As soon as a female butterfly mates, it uses chemical cues to find the appropriate plant upon which to lay its eggs. Unless there is an assortment of suitable larval food in your garden, the butterflies

❧ Flower shape is also important. Most butterflies prefer single tubular blooms that stand up straight, are easy to land on and have easily accessible nectar. A butterfly draws nectar by inserting its tube-shape mouth, or proboscis, into the flower. Butterflies are also rather lazy and prefer flowers in clusters which they can visit in one stop; flat-topped clusters and large-lipped flowers — such as most of the daisy family, with tiny flowers packed into a flat head — provide a landing strip and allow butterflies to perch and relax as they feed.

❧ When selecting cultivated species of plants, choose old-fashioned varieties over the newer cultivars since their fragrance is stronger and their nectar production greater.

❧ The site of your garden can also affect your success at attracting butterflies, since shelter and basking sites are as critical as food. Butterflies are cold-blooded and need a place to bask in the sun in order to maintain the high body temperature they need to fly — so a sunny garden

that you've lured to your garden with nectar plants won't be encouraged to stay and propagate.

While adult butterflies thrive on a variety of nectar-rich flowers, the diet of the larvae is much more limited — and dependent on another group of plants (see list, next page). Unfortunately, some of these plants are considered weeds and are not attractive additions to the garden. Keep them under control by planting them in buried pots and removing flower heads to prevent rampant self-seeding.

To protect more desirable garden plants from possible caterpillar damage, it's a good idea to include a few feed or larva plants in out-of-the-way spots in the garden. If you notice any caterpillars chewing on your garden plants, you can transfer them by hand to suitable feed plants. Or simply let them be; most caterpillars do not settle on plants in sufficient numbers to do them harm.

A LURE *for* BUTTERFLIES

Most species of butterflies require very specific larval foods but a broader range of nectar foods. In order to attract as many butterflies as possible to your garden, offer a variety of both.

Common Milkweed (Asclepias syriaca)

FOR NECTAR

❧ The best-known butterfly flower is the common milkweed (*Asclepias syricacus*), host of the graceful orange and black monarch butterfly found throughout much of Canada. Although its flowers are moderately attractive, its heavy, awkward foliage yellows early in the season, making it a poor choice for some garden settings. A related species, the butterfly weed (*Asclepias tuberosa*), has thinner, less objectionable foliage and long-lasting flowers in bright shades of orange, red and yellow. Easy to grow and available through many seed houses.

it thrives in dry or poor soil and attracts a wide variety of butterflies.

❧ Popular spring-flowering plants include primroses (*Primula*), rock cress (*Aubrieta* and *Arabis*), candytuft (*Iberis*) and biennial sweet William (*Dianthus barbatus*).

❧ If it's dependable in your area (some varieties are hardy to Zone 5), lavender (*Lavendula*) is an excellent choice for early-summer bloom.

❧ Butterfly flowers for summer include bee balm (*Monarda*), tickweed (*Coreopsis*), foxglove (*Digitalis*), gayfeather (*Liatris*), heliotrope (*Heliotropium arborescens*), hollyhock (*Alcea rosea*), lupine (*Lupinus*), mallow (*Malva*), mignonette (*Reseda odorata*), orange daylily (*Hemerocallis fulva*), pearly everlasting (*Anaphalis margaritacea*), pincushion (*Scabiosa*), sunflower (*Helianthus*) and vervain (*Verbena*). Most daisy-like flowers, especially those with yellow centers, are also good choices — as are clover (*Melilotus*) and bird's-foot trefoil (*Lotus corniculatus*).

❧ Purple coneflower (*Echinacea purpurea*) is one of the best native wildflowers, as is ironweed (*Veronica*) and Joe-pyeweed (*Eupatorium purpureum*).

❧ Long-blooming, nectar-rich annuals include marigolds, zinnias, salvia, vervain (*Verbena*), sweet alyssum (*Lobularia maritima*) and lantana.

❧ For fall, showy stonecrop (*Sedum spectabile*) is a good choice because of its long-lasting flowers. The native New England aster (*Aster novae-angliae*) is another good fall nectar plant, as are border phlox (*Phlox paniculata*) and goldenrod (*Solidago*).

❧ The butterfly bush (*Buddleia davidii*) blooms from midsummer to October with clusters of fragrant pink, purple or white flowers. It's excellent for attracting a wide range of species, including red admirals, painted ladies, Milbert's tortoise shell and fritillaries.

❧ Lastly, don't forget about trees and shrubs. Lilacs (*Syringa*) attract mourning cloaks and swallowtails; red admirals enjoy the nectar of the wild cherry.

FOR LARVAL FOOD

The following lists some of Canada's most popular butterflies, along with the specific food plants their caterpillars enjoy.

❧ EASTERN BLACK SWALLOWTAIL — wild carrot, parsley, celery, Queen Anne's lace

❧ EASTERN TIGER SWALLOWTAIL — tulip tree, black cherry, birch

❧ SPICEBUSH SWALLOWTAIL — sassafras and spicebush

❧ FRITILLARIES — violets

❧ COMMAS AND RED ADMIRALS — stinging nettle

❧ NORTHERN BALTIMORE — turtlehead

❧ MONARCH — milkweed

❧ SKIPPERS — hollyhocks, ornamental grasses

❧ PAINTED LADY — Canada thistle and bull thistle, hollyhocks

❧ SULPHURS — clover

❧ QUESTION MARK — elms

❧ MOURNING CLOAK — elms, willow, poplars

❧ RED-SPOTTED PURPLE — black cherry, poplar, gooseberry, willow

❧ SPRING AZURE — meadowsweet

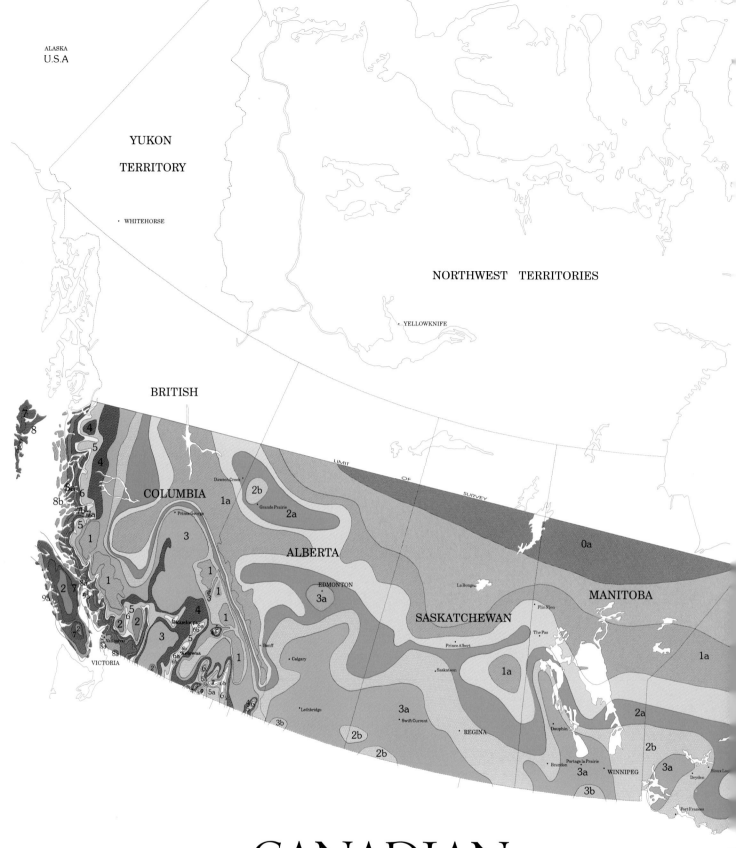

CANADIAN
PLANT HARDINESS
ZONE MAP

This map shows the areas of winter hardiness for ornamental plants in the more heavily populated areas of Canada. The map is based on a formula that takes into consideration several meteorological factors affecting the hardiness of a plant in a given location.

The most important element in plant survival is the minimum temperature during the winter. Other important considerations are the length of the frost-free period, summer rainfall, maximum temperatures, snow cover and wind.

The hardiness areas have been divided into 10 zones. The one marked 0 is the coldest. Other zones are progressively milder, to 9, which is the mildest. A given zone on this map corresponds only approximately to a zone of the same number in the United States Department of Agriculture Plant Hardiness Zone Map, which has been in use in Canada for a number of years. This map, however, presents more detail for Canada.

If data warranted it, each zone was subdivided into a dark and a light section to represent, respectively, the colder and milder portions of the zone. If undivided, the zone was designated by the color of the colder section.

LABRADOR

QUEBEC

NEWFOUNDLAND

ST JOHN'S

Gander

Corner Brook

4b

3b

5b

5a

5b

6a

5a

P.E.I.

CHARLOTTETOWN

Sydney

Baie Comeau

Chibougamau

2

Campbellton

NEW BRUNSWICK

Edmundston

3b

3a

4a

FREDERICTON

Moncton

5b

5a

NOVA SCOTIA

1b

0

1a

Timmins

Noranda

QUEBEC

Trois-Rivières

3a

1b

5a

St. John

HALIFAX

6a

Yarmouth

6b

Sudbury

Montreal

OTTAWA

5a

4b

Kingston

5b

Lake Huron

Barrie

5b

Lake Ontario

4b

TORONTO

7a

London

6a

6b

Lake Erie

Windsor

7a

7b

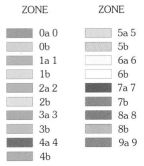

LEGEND

NOTE: Darker tint indicates colder part, lighter tint of same color indicates milder part.

ZONE	ZONE
0a 0	5a 5
0b	5b
1a 1	6a 6
1b	6b
2a 2	7a 7
2b	7b
3a 3	8a 8
3b	8b
4a 4	9a 9
4b	

RESOURCE MATERIAL

CANADIAN NATIVE PLANT SOCIETIES *and* SOURCES *of* INFORMATION

The Canadian Wildflower Society
4981 Highway 7 East, Unit 12A, Suite 228,
Markham, Ontario L3R 1N1

The Canadian Wildflower Society,
Wellington/Waterloo Chapter
c/o Allan Anderson, Botany Department, University
of Guelph, Guelph, Ontario N1G 2W1

The Canadian Wildflower Society, London Chapter
665 Windemere Road, Suite 711, London,
Ontario N5X 2Y6

The Canadian Wildflower Society,
Newfoundland Chapter
633 Pouch Cove Highway, Flat Rock,
Newfoundland A1K 1C8

The Canadian Wildflower Society,
Nova Scotia Wild Flora Society
c/o Nova Scotia Museum, 1747 Summer Street,
Halifax, Nova Scotia N3H 3A6

The U.B.C. Botanical Garden
6501 NW Marine Drive,
The University of British Columbia,
Vancouver, BC V6T 1W5

Living Prairie Museum
2795 Ness Avenue, Winnipeg,
Manitoba R3J 3S4

Drought-Resistant Plants

One of the best ways to cut down on water use in the garden is to rely on native plants and on hardy perennials and annuals with low water needs. All of the plants listed below thrive nicely with the prevailing rainfall and little more.

TREES

- Colorado spruce
  (*Picea pungens*)
- Common juniper
  (*Juniperus communis*)
- Goldenrain tree
  (*Koelreuteria*)
- Hackberry
  (*Celtis*)
- Honey locust
  (*Gleditsia*)
- Jack pine
  (*Pinus banksiana*)
- Lodgepole pine
  (*P. contorta latifolia*)
- Red pine
  (*P. resinosa*)
- Russian olive
  (*Elaeagnus angustifolia*)
- Tatarian maple
  (*Acer tatarica*)
- Tree of heaven
  (*Ailanthus altissima*)

SHRUBS

- Adam's needle
  (*Yucca filamentosa*)
- Alder buckthorn
  (*Rhamnus frangula*)
- Broom
  (*Cytissus*)
- Buffalo berry
  (*Shepherdia argentea*)
- Cinquefoil
  (*Potentilla*)
- Flowering quince
  (*Chaenomeles*)
- Firethorn
  (*Pyracantha*)
- Grey dogwood
  (*Cornus racemosa*)
- Peashrub
  (*Caragana*)
- Silverberry
  (*Elaeagnus commutatus*)
- Sumac
  (*Rhus*)

GROUND COVERS

- Bearberry
  (*Arctostaphylos uva-ursi*)
- Chamomile
  (*Anthemis tinctoria*)
- Creeping juniper
  (*Juniperus horizontalis*)
- Crown vetch
  (*Coronilla varia*)
- Orpine
  (*Sedum*)
- Sagebrush
  (*Artemisia*)
- Thyme
  (*Thymus*)
- Wild ginger
  (*Asarum*)

PERENNIALS

- Aster
- Black-eyed Susan
  (*Rudbeckia hirta*)
- Butterfly weed
  (*Asclepias tuberosa*)
- Candytuft
  (*Iberis*)
- Coreopsis
- Globe thistle
  (*Echinops*)
- Goldenrod
  (*Solidago*)
- Lamb's-ears
  (*Stachys byzantina*)
- Lavender
- Moss pink
  (*Phlox subulata*)
- Oriental poppy
  (*Papaver orientale*)
- Penstomen
- Spurge
  (*Euphorbia*)
- Yarrow
  (*Achillea*)

ANNUALS

- Calendula
- Cosmos
  (*C. bipinnatus*)
- Gazania
  (*G. rigens*)
- Globe amaranth
  (*Gomphrena globosa*)
- Marigold
  (*Tagetes* spp.)
- Portulaca
  (*P. grandiflora*)
- Statice
  (*Limonium sinuatum*)
- Strawflower
  (*Helichrysum bracteatum*)

NATIVE GRASSES

- Big bluestem
  (*Andropogon gerardii*)
- Little bluestem
  (*A. scoparius*)
- Meadow fescue
  (*Festuca elatior*)
- Needlegrass
  (*Stipa spartea*)
- Side oats gramma
  (*Bouteloua curtipendula*)
- Switchgrass
  (*Panicum virgatum*)
- Wild oats
  (*Chasmantheum latifolium*)

ORNAMENTAL GRASSES
(for use as accent plants)

- Blue oat grass
  (*Helictotrichon sempervirens*)
- European feather grass
  (*Stipa pennata*)
- Feather reed grass
  (*Calamagrostis acutiflora*)
- Quaking grass
  (*Briza media*)
- Tufted hairgrass
  (*Deschampsia caespitosa*)

Plants *for* Wettish Soils

SHRUBS

- Black chokeberry
  (*Aronia melanocarpa*)
- Buttonbush
  (*Cephalanthus*)
- Common witch hazel
  (*Hamamelis virginiana*)
- Elderberry
  (*Sambucus*)
- Mountain laurel
  (*Kalmia*)
- Red osier dogwood
  (*Cornus stolonifera*)
- Summersweet
  (*Clethra alnifolia*)
- Winterberry
  (*Ilex verticillata*)

TREES

- American larch
  (*Larix laricina*)
- Bald cypress
  (*Taxodium disticum*)
- Black ash
  (*Fraxinus nigra*)
- Common alder
  (*Alnus glutinosa*)
- Hackberry
  (*Celtis*)
- Pin oak
  (*Quercus palustris*)
- Swamp white oak
  (*Q. bicolor*)
- Red maple
  (*Acer rubrum*)
- River birch
  (*Betula nigra*)
- Yellow birch
  (*B. alleghaniensis*)
- White spruce
  (*Picea glauca*)
- Willow
  (*Salix*)

PERENNIALS

- Astilbe
- Bee balm
  (*Monarda didyma*)
- Cardinal flower
  (*Lobelia cardinalis*)
- Coral bells
  (*Heuchera*)
- Daylily
  (*Hemerocallis*)
- Giant groundsel
  (*Ligularia*)
- Globeflower
  (*Trollius*)
- Gooseneck
  (*Lysimachia clethroides*)
- Hosta
- Meadowsweet
  (*Filipendula ulmeria*)
- Primrose
  (*Primula*)
- Siberian iris
  (*Iris sibirica*)
- Skunk cabbage
  (*Lysichitum americanum*)
- Turtlehead
  (*Chelone obliqua*)

ANNUALS

- Baby-blue-eyes
  (*Nemophila menziesii*)
- Monkey flower
  (*Mimulus*)
- Patience plant
  (*Impatiens*)
- Rose balsam
  (*Impatiens balsamina*)
- Wax begonia
  (*Begonia semperflorens*)

NATIVE GRASSES

- Big bluestem
  (*Andropogon gerardii*)
- Fox sedge
  (*Carex vulpinoidea*)
- Switchgrass
  (*Panicum virgatum*)
  — but this tends to be aggressive in moist soils.

ORNAMENTAL GRASSES
(for use as accent plants)

- Fountain grass
  (*Pennisetum alopecuroides*)
- Gardener's garters
  (*Phalaris arundinacea*)
- Gray's sedge
  (*Carex grayi*)
- Japanese silver grass
  (*Miscanthus sinensis*)
- Northern sea oat
  (*Chasmanthium latifolium*)
- Purple moor grass
  (*Molinia arundinacea*)

GROUND COVERS

- Bugleweed
  (*Ajuga reptans*)
- Cutleaf stephanandra
  (*Stephanandra incisa*)
- False spirea
  (*Sorbaria sorbifolia*)

THE CONTRIBUTORS

LIZ PRIMEAU is the editor of *Canadian Gardening*. In her five years with the magazine, she has visited gardens in all parts of Canada and has heard firsthand from committed Canadian gardeners about what works — or doesn't work! — in this widely varied climate of ours. An avid and experienced gardener herself, she has also been a featured speaker at gardening conferences, trade shows and garden clubs. Liz Primeau writes regularly on gardening for *The Globe and Mail's* Design section, and has also worked as a writer and editor with *Weekend Magazine*, *Toronto Life*, *Chatelaine*, *City Woman*, *Vista* and *Ontario Living* during a 23-year journalistic career.

TREVOR AND BRENDA COLE met as horticultural students at the Royal Botanical Gardens, Kew, in England. After graduating, they worked in several parks departments and nurseries before emigrating to Canada in 1967. Trevor then worked for Agriculture Canada as Curator of the Dominion Arboretum, retiring in 1995. He has also written two books — *The Ontario Gardener* (1991) and *Gardening with Trees and Shrubs* (spring 1996). Brenda is a freelance garden writer, with a regular column in *The Ottawa Citizen* and the *North Bay Nugget*. Together they write a column of regional news for *Canadian Gardening* magazine.

FRANK KERSHAW has taught gardening courses at the Civic Garden Centre in Toronto and at the Royal Botanical Gardens in Hamilton, Ontario, and has lectured widely on gardening topics in Canada, the United States and in other countries. Over the last ten years, he has led numerous garden tours and has visited and photographed over 300 gardens in North America, the Caribbean and Europe. Frank Kershaw is director of planning, research and construction for the Metropolitan Toronto Parks and Culture Department which administers some 4,600 hectares of regional open space.

Photographers

DAN CALLIS: page 67.

TREVOR COLE: pages 34, 38, 64, 65, 84.

CHRISTOPHER DEW: back cover (right); pages 3, 33, 80.

TURID FORSYTH: pages 4, 6, 18 (bottom), 22 (top), 46, 49, 51, 72, 73, 75 (top), 77, 82, 85.

ALEX GAILITIS: back cover (left); pages 7, 22 (bottom), 23 (bottom), 24 (bottom), 28, 47 (bottom), 58, 61 (right), 63 (bottom), 66.

JIM HODGINS: pages 12, 13, 17 (bottom right), 18 (middle), 47 (top), 50 (inset), 53 (middle and bottom), 56, 59, 62, 63 (top), 75 (bottom left).

DAVID INGLIS: pages 10, 54, 57, 61 (left), 83.

FRANK KERSHAW: pages 9, 11, 14, 16, 17 (top and bottom left), 18 (top), 19, 21, 24 (top), 25, 27, 30, 31, 36, 37, 45, 48 (top), 52, 56, 63 (middle), 74, 75 (bottom right).

BERT KLASSEN: photo of Liz Primeau; pages 8, 20.

JOI IN MORRISON: front cover; pages 48 (bottom), 68.

JERRY SHULMAN: pages 42, 69 (top), 71 (top), 76 (top), 78, 79, 81.

LYNN THOMPSON: title page; pages 69 (bottom), 70 (background), 71 (bottom), 76 (bottom).

DAVID TOMLINSON: page 39.

ZILE ZICHMANIS: pages 15, 23 (top), 44, 50 (background), 60.

ANONYMOUS: pages 43, 53 (top), 70 (inset).

The Canadian Plant Hardiness Zone Map (pages 86-87) was produced by the Centre for Land and Biological Resources Research, Research Branch, Agriculture Canada, from information supplied by the Ottawa Research Station and the Meteorological Branch, Environment Canada 1993. ❧ We would like to thank Bryan Monette and Ron St. John of the Research Branch for their kind help in supplying us with this material.

Acknowledgments

We are grateful to the many talented garden writers from across the country whose articles in *Canadian Gardening* magazine over the last six years have been an inspiration for this book series. For this book in particular, we would like to thank Veronica Healy Colangelo, Trevor and Brenda Cole, Rebecca Hanes-Fox, Larry Hodgson, David Inglis, Frank Kershaw and Jake MacDonald. ❧ We are also indebted to Jim Hodgins and Zile Zichmanis of the Canadian Wildflower Society for their kind assistance with this project, and for the invaluable photos they supplied.

SPECIAL THANKS

❧ Many people deserve my heartfelt thanks for their help in the preparation of this book. Wanda Nowakowska, Madison Press project editor, first — I can't begin to tell you of the midnight oil she burned and the energy she devoted to the successful completion of the book. She deserves a medal. So do our consultants, Frank Kershaw and Trevor and Brenda Cole — we'd be lost without their expertise and their basic, common-sense understanding of natural gardens. Rebecca Hanes-Fox, *Canadian Gardening* managing editor, was a constant support with her ideas and her superb editing of the manuscript. Gord Sibley's elegant design gives the book the class we like, as do the photographs provided by many of the magazine's contributors. I am also indebted to Tom Hopkins, the magazine's editorial director, for his ongoing encouragement and enthusiasm, and to our publisher, Phil Whalen, for his commitment to the series.   — *Liz Primeau*

Selected Bibliography

❧ Davis, Rosalie H. "Butterfly Gardening." *Horticulture*, June 1989: 50-53.

❧ Druse, Ken. *The Natural Garden.* New York: Clarkson N. Potter, Inc., 1989.

❧ Hodgins, James, and Frank Kershaw. "Wildflower Gardening: The Great Lakes and the Northeast Atlantic Region." Unpublished manuscript.

❧ Lamb, Larry. "Attracting Wildlife to Your Garden."

❧ Lord, Jack. "Gardening for Butterflies." The Gardens' Bulletin, from PAPPUS Vol.6, No.1, Summer 1986: 14-16.

❧ Stolzenburg, William. "Silent Sirens." *Wildflower*, Summer 1993: 18-22.

INDEX

I

Ilex
    I. glabra, 74
    I. verticillata, 74, *75*
Iliamna rivularis, 50
Immigrant plants, 5
Impatiens capensis, 79
Imperata 'Red Baron', 65, *65*
Indian grass, 60, *60*
Inkberry, 74
Insecticides, 69
Insects, 43, 58, 81
    beneficial, 6, 69
Ipomoea
    I. coccinea, 79
    I. purpurea, 79
Iris
    dwarf crested, 16
    I. cristata, 16

J

Jack-in-the-pulpit, 10, 16, 24, *24*, 26
Jacob's ladder, 26
Japanese blood grass, 65, *65*
Japanese flowering quince, 79
Japanese holly fern, 29
Japanese painted fern, 27
Japanese red shield fern, 29
Japanese yellow bellflower, 28
Jewelweed, 79
Job's tears, 65
June grass, 60

K

Kirengeshoma palmata, 28
Koeleria cristata, 60
Kolkwitzia amabilis, 79

L

Lady beetles, 81
Lady's mantle, 26
Lamium, 78
Larkspur, 56, 76
Leaf mulches, 20, 28
Leguminosae, 54
Leucojum aestivum, 35, 39

Liatris
    L. punctata, 62
    L. spicata, 47, *47*, *53*
Ligustrum, 78
Lilac, 78
Lilium, 50
    L. columbianum, 51
    L. martagon, 35
    L. philadelphicum, 44, *44*, 47
Lily-of-the-valley, 24, *24*
Linnaea borealis, 23, *23*
Linum perenne var. *lewisii*, 50, *51*
Lithospermum croceum, 63, *63*
Little bluestem, 60
Lobelia
    L. cardinalis, 47, *47*, 78
    L. spicata, 61
Lonicera, 73
    L. X brownii 'Dropmore Scarlet', 78
Love-lies-bleeding, 76
Lupinus (Lupine), 10, *54*, 54-55, 61, 83, *83*
    Silky, 55
    Tree, 55
    L. arboreus, 55
    L. perennis, 55
    L. polyphyllus, 55
    L. sericeus, 55

M

Magnolia, 34
Mahonia aquifolium, 29
Maianthemum canadense, 17
Malva alcea fastigiata, 26
Marigold, 76
Marsh marigolds, 10
Matteuccia struthiopteris, 26, 27, 28
Mayapple, *14*, 18, *18*, 19
Meadow rue, 26
Meadows, 9, 10, 40-55
    creating your own, 43
    definition, 43
    flowers, *4*, 6, *7*, *11*, *40*, *42*, 46-53, *49*
    grasses, 43, 44
    ideal sites, 43
    planting, 44, 45
    plants, 43
    preparing the site, 44, 45
    small properties, 43
    when to plant, 44
Mertensia virginica, 22, *22*, 26, 79

Mice, 35, 38
Milkweed
    common, 85, *85*
    white woodland, 24
Millium effusum, 65
Mirabilis, 76, 79
Miscanthus sinensis, 64, *64*
Mitchella repens, 74
Monarda didyma, 48, 49, 78
Monarda fistulosa, 49, 51
Morning-glory, 79
Moss rose, 76
Moths, 53, 81
Mountain mint, 48
Mulches, 21
    leaf, 20, 28
Muscari, 18, 31, *33*, 35, 38
Myosotis scorpioides, 26

N

Narcissus, 30, 37, *37*
    miniature, 38
Nasturtium, 79
Native plants, 5, 9
Natural elements, 69
Natural gardening
    definition, 5, 9
    habitats for wildlife, 68-69
    movement, 5
Needle grass, 60
Nepeta, 78
New England aster, 49
Nicotiana, 78
Nodding pink onion, 61
Northern bedstraw, 43
Northern sea oat, 64, *64*

O

Obedient plant, 48
Oenothera
    O. biennis, 53
    O. fruticosa, *52*, 53
Onoclea sensibilis, 27, 29
Oregon grape, 29
Ornamental grasses, 9, 44, 64-65, *64-65*
Osmunda
    O. cinnamomomea, 29
    O. claytoniana, 27, 29
    O. regalis, 28
Oxalis oregana, 23

P

Pacific dogwood, 17
Pale-spike lobelia, 61
Parasitic wasps, 81
Parthenocissus quinquefolia, 74, *74*
Partridgeberry, 74
Pasqueflower, 60, 63, *63*
Paths, 9, 21
    mown grass, 9
    wood-chip, 9
Pearly everlasting, 53, *53*
Pennisetum setaceum, 65, *65*
Penstemon, 78, 79
    P. digitalis, 47, 53
Pest control, 10
Pests, woodland, 21, 35
Petalostemum purpureum, 61, *61*
Petunia, 76, *78*, 79
Phalaris arundinacea, 64, 65
Phaseolus coccineus, 79
Phlox, 76, 79
    P. divaricata, 16, 22, *22*
Physostegia virginiana, 48
Pines, 73
    eastern white, 73
    red, 73
Pinks, 76
Pinus
    P. resinosa, 73
    P. strobus, 73
Podophyllum peltatum, *14*, 18, *18*
Polemonium caeruleum, 26
Polystichum
    P. acrostichoides, 27, 28
    P. angulare, 29
    P. braunii, 27
    P. munitum, 27, 29
Ponds, 21, 35
Portulaca, 76
Pot marigold, 76
Prairie crocus, *41*, 58, 60, 63, *63*
Prairie dropseed, 60
Prairie gardens, 56-63
    maintenance, 58
    preparation, 58
    sowing, 58
Prairie smoke, 60, 62, *62*, 63
Prairie willow, 58
Prairie yellow violet, 61

EDITORIAL DIRECTOR Hugh Brewster

PROJECT EDITOR Wanda Nowakowska

EDITORIAL ASSISTANCE Rebecca Hanes-Fox

PRODUCTION DIRECTOR Susan Barrable

PRODUCTION COORDINATOR Sandra L. Hall

BOOK DESIGN AND LAYOUT Gordon Sibley Design Inc.

PRINTING AND BINDING Tien Wah Press

CANADIAN GARDENING'S
NATURAL GARDENS
was produced by
Madison Press Books